"A compelling exploration of how a piece of cloth can transform your role in the fabric of society. Nadeine Asbali skilfully navigates the complex interplay between fear, bias and security policies like Prevent to unveil the Islamophobia faced by visibly Muslim women and the demonisation of an entire community. From counter-terrorism to Turkey Twizzlers, this book enlightens and entertains simultaneously."

Dr Layla Aitlhadj, director of Prevent Watch

"*Veiled Threat* is more of an invitation than a threat. Nadeine Asbali presents, through vignettes of her life, some of the most pertinent and universal flashpoints in the lives of British Muslims. She expertly handles the varying issues of heritage, identity, Islam, racism, feminism, humanity, motherhood and even joy with thoughtfulness and insight. Despite some of the heavier topics covered, Nadeine's unique narrative style makes this an enjoyable whilst informative read. An essential addition to school curricula and home libraries."

Dr Sofia Rehman, author of *A Treasury of 'A'ishah*

"As a visible Muslim and a dedicated doctor, *Veiled Threat* is a refreshing and eloquent testament to the nuanced challenges faced by Muslim women and men in modern-day Britain. Nadeine Asbali's enquiries into the intricate intersections of misogyny and Islamophobia provide a profound understanding of the unique burdens borne by Muslim women, illustrating the systemic and institutional biases that disproportionately affect us. Her critique of white feminism is a vital contribution to the discourse on intersectionality, encouraging readers to engage in meaningful conversations about inclusivity and solidarity within the feminist movement. In addition, Nadeine's exploration of social class as a compounding factor in experiences of Islamophobia enriches the narrative, painting a comprehensive picture of the challenges faced by Muslims across different socio-economic strata. This book not only resonates with my personal experiences but also advances the discourse on diversity, inclusion and the intricate intersections of Muslim identity. A must-read for anybody passionate about creating a more inclusive and informed society, promoting dialogue and solidarity across diverse communities."

Dr Kiran Rahim, paediatrician and Instagram educator

"A powerful journey into the complexities of identity and visibility as a Muslim woman in contemporary Britain. Nadeine Asbali, with poignant honesty, explores the impact of societal expectations and the intersectionality of Islamophobia and misogyny. Through vivid anecdotes and incisive observations, *Veiled Threat* challenges stereotypes, exposing the struggle of being perceived as an outsider in one's own home. It's a compelling study of resilience, sisterhood and the profound influence of the hijab on one's sense of self."

Rabina Khan, writer and former Liberal Democrat councillor

VEILED THREAT

ON BEING VISIBLY MUSLIM IN BRITAIN

NADEINE ASBALI

\Bb\
Biteback Publishing

First published in Great Britain in 2024 by
Biteback Publishing Ltd, London
Copyright © Nadeine Asbali 2024

Nadeine Asbali has asserted her right under the Copyright, Designs and Patents Act 1988 to be identified as the author of this work.

All rights reserved. No part of this publication may be reproduced, stored in a retrieval system or transmitted, in any form or by any means, without the publisher's prior permission in writing.

This book is sold subject to the condition that it shall not, by way of trade or otherwise, be lent, resold, hired out or otherwise circulated without the publisher's prior consent in any form of binding or cover other than that in which it is published and without a similar condition, including this condition, being imposed on the subsequent purchaser.

Every reasonable effort has been made to trace copyright holders of material reproduced in this book, but if any have been inadvertently overlooked the publisher would be glad to hear from them.

ISBN 978-1-78590-819-4

10 9 8 7 6 5 4 3 2 1

A CIP catalogue record for this book is available from the British Library.

Set in Minion Pro and Interstate

Printed and bound in Great Britain by
CPI Group (UK) Ltd, Croydon CR0 4YY

In the name of Allah, the most beneficent, the most merciful.

This book is for my sisters in faith, my fellow visibly Muslim women. Those, like me, whose existence is built upon the precarious ground of policy and stereotype, penned in between the twin oppressions of misogyny and Islamophobia, our voices drowned out by the endless din of those seeking to save us and others condemning our covered bodies as foreign, menacing, un-British. This is for us: we whose very presence on this racist island is resistance. Here's to refusing to be fetishised, maligned and criminalised into integrating, into belonging. Here's to refusing to prove our humanity to white feminists who trample over our dead bodies, politicians who call us letter boxes and a nation that never bothers to see us as anything but meek victims, convenient political mascots and veiled threats all at once.

'The woman who sees without being seen frustrates the coloniser.'
FRANTZ FANON

CONTENTS

Introduction — 1

Chapter 1   Turkey Twizzlers and couscous on Sundays — 7
English, Libyan, other

Chapter 2   Blood, bone and chiffon — 23
How the hijab changed everything

Chapter 3   Central reservations — 53
The dichotomy facing Muslim women

Chapter 4   Sinister saviours — 85
White feminism (and other lies)

Chapter 5   Letter boxes — 115
How Islamophobia in Britain is gendered

Chapter 6   Invisible — 139
Mothering whilst Muslim

Chapter 7   Muslim masculinity — 165
Andrew Tate, Mincels and the akh-right

Chapter 8	A nation within a nation	197
	How class compounds Islamophobia in Britain	
Chapter 9	Bottom of the class	221
	Being Muslim in an education system that excludes us	
Chapter 10	Salaams and smiles	247
	What the hijab gave me	

Conclusion		269
Acknowledgements		273

INTRODUCTION

I'd be the first to say that a scarf on a woman's head doesn't define her, but in my case it's a lie.

My racialisation occurred overnight. One day I was a white(ish) child with a slightly foreign-sounding surname and the next I was something sinister and threatening, perverse and foreign. Suddenly, I was an outsider in the town I called home. I was called 'Taliban' on the bus and grown adults steered their children away from my covered head as though my otherness was contagious, like the flu. Teachers swooped in to save me from the chauvinistic father they imagined to be the cause of my newly covered hair. I didn't know it as a mixed-race teenager, but I had been passing as white my whole life. My passably English-sounding first name, my white mother and my homelife of Turkey Twizzlers and *Tracy Beaker* had sold me the myth that I was like anyone else – that I had access to Britishness by birthright. That it could never get taken away.

But then the façade, and the entire life I had built upon its premise, collapsed. No longer a normal kid who went under the radar, I learned that being visibly Muslim in a nation as hostile as Britain means forever living in the margins. A perpetual victim, a ceaseless threat. The object of someone's fetish or someone else's white saviour complex. A political symbol, a harbinger of extremism. A terrorist's wife or a woman desperate to whip off her headscarf. Never, ever simply ourselves.

Still, I almost didn't write this book.

I thought, *it's so rudimentary, isn't it?* So obvious. So typical. A hijabi writing about the hijab, as though the only thing Muslim women are capable of writing about is what's on our heads rather than anything that might happen to be inside them.

I wondered if anyone would care about what a Muslim woman had to say about a piece of cloth. I doubted if the things I had to say were even relevant any more. *Look around you*, I told myself, there's a hijabi in pretty much every make-up advert on TV these days. Nadiya Hussain is a household name. Primark puts headscarves on its mannequins. I haven't been asked by a student if Muslims are 'the ones who shoot everyone' in at least half a decade. Let it go!

But that's the point. Muslims shouldn't have to prove our humanity, our worth. We shouldn't have to win gold medals or baking contests to matter. We shouldn't have to

INTRODUCTION

fold ourselves up and squeeze through the narrow definitions that society dictates of us in order to be heard. We shouldn't have to dress a certain way, behave a certain way, think a certain way in order for people to listen up.

Well, this is me forcing you to listen. I may be a Muslim woman but I don't speak for us all, so if you have come to this book for representation – to tick your book club's diversity box for the month – look away. I am tired of defending, explaining, justifying my existence away. I am exhausted from constantly condemning actions that aren't mine, obscuring parts of me that are unpalatable to the only place I have called home. This book is not about what all Muslim women think; but it *is* about what it means to be visibly foreign in a nation intent on forced assimilation and integration, that views covered bodies as primitive and dangerous. It *is* about grappling the twin oppressions of misogyny and Islamophobia, and how Muslim women are perpetually stuck between patriarchal cultural norms in our own communities, racist policy-making, white saviour feminism and the unstoppable Islamophobia machine. And it is about the gleaming joys to be found in those margins, too. The sisterhood, the community. The beauty, the fulfilment. It is about all the ways the hijab has defined me – for better and for worse.

As I wrote this book, Muslim women were suddenly back in the news again. In the past few months alone, France has banned girls from wearing anything even remotely

Muslim-looking in state schools – including co-ord sets and high-street maxi dresses. Palestinian women are giving birth in bombed-out hospitals with no anaesthetic whilst the world sanctions it as self-defence. France (yes, again) has just prohibited its athletes from wearing the hijab during the upcoming 2024 Paris Olympics, and we're over a year on from white feminists saving Muslim women in Iran by livestreaming themselves shaving their heads. The spectre of a British Prime Minister referring to us as 'letter boxes' hangs over our heads. The name Shamima is practically a racist slur. And the world's most viral misogynist has become a Muslim and converted scores of our brothers, husbands and sons to the idea that we are subhuman.

From Europeans colonising the mysterious, primitive 'east' full of sensual veiled women being traded for camels to today, where wearing an H&M maxi dress to a French school is illegal if your name is Khadija but not Chloe, Muslim women have come no further in unshackling ourselves from the double jeopardy of Islamophobia and misogyny. The same old myths, stereotypes and paradoxes that have always defined us still prevail, confining us in ways that, ironically, we are told only the scarves on our heads are to blame for.

So, to answer my own question: yes. Writing about the hijab does matter now as much as it ever has done. Perhaps more. I can't imagine an archetype of visible foreignness more contested and political than the hijab and thinking

INTRODUCTION

about what it means to be visibly Muslim in Britain is to get to the very core of the Islamophobia, misogyny and racism that rules our society. It is to expose how state surveillance, geopolitics and social expectation compete on the battleground of our bodies. It is to interrogate liberalism's unshakable hatred of covered bodies. It is to hold this nation to account for what it does to those who don't assimilate. To say, I'd rather be a *veiled threat* than your version of a palatable Muslim woman.

CHAPTER 1

TURKEY TWIZZLERS AND COUSCOUS ON SUNDAYS

ENGLISH, LIBYAN, OTHER

My mum called me down for dinner in that sing-song way she always did. But I was busy.

Nade-eine, dinner's rea-dy – she called again, as I illustrated the hundredth perfectly placed eyelash and traced the curve of a nose on the two faces peering up at me from the pages of my sketchbook.

Dinner's getting cold, sweetheart, she said, now in my room. A dab of blue eyeshadow here. A fringe there.

What are you drawing?

It's me, Mummy.

Which one?

Both.

…

Come on, sweetie, let's eat.

I know what you're thinking: this memory sounds made up. It's just almost *too* convenient to be real. It *too* perfectly conveys the fragmented and fractured innards of my identity to sound like something a kid would actually do. But that's why it's real – because I really did view myself as two separate but simultaneous beings. I simply didn't know how to be both.

One version of me had long flowing hair and bare shoulders, sometimes with a little star tattoo. This me had long lacquered lashes, cat eyeliner to rival Cleopatra's and a Barbie doll pout. The other me had my head covered in an eclectically patterned scarf with a spherical face in a permanently chirpy smile. One was the English me and one was the Libyan me. On the brink of adulthood, I would become one, but I was never quite sure which one that would be. Like a caterpillar awaiting the chrysalis, I didn't yet know what I'd emerge as.

Before becoming a visibly Muslim woman with an awareness of the heavy political implications of my existence, I was just a child with a foreign-sounding surname and skin that tanned easily. Growing up with an English, non-Muslim mother and a Libyan, Muslim father was like having two selves that lived parallel lives inside of me. These two sides of me barely met, and so they co-existed perfectly. Like flatmates who work opposite shifts, one sleeping whilst the other lives their life. Experiencing nothing of each other except some crumbs on the worktop and the scent of perfume lingering by the door. The eldest child in a mixed-race home has no blueprint for how to navigate life between two identities. I was making it up as I went along, and the way I dealt with it was to separate the fractions of my being along physical, geographical and temporal lines.

On weekdays, I was English. I wrote song lyrics up my arm and ate Turkey Twizzlers in front of *The Simpsons* (followed by *The Weakest Link*). I did my homework at the table and pretended I wasn't listening to *Hollyoaks* in the background and spoke to my friends on MSN about who said what about whom. I wrapped my hair in socks so it would be curly for school and begged my mum to let me walk to the shop on my own for sweets. I listened to my iPod at the dinner table by hiding the earphones behind my hair and thought slamming my bedroom door in anger was the most grown-up thing in the world. I stayed up past my bedtime reading *Harry Potter* under my duvet and painted my nails a different colour on every finger.

Then, I was Libyan when we'd hurtle up the M1 every weekend to meet my dad's old Libyan school friends in Coventry, Nottingham and Sheffield. I was Libyan when we'd eat stuffed peppers on kitchen floors, the lost cadence of Arabic washing over me as we listened to our dads rally against the dictatorship they had all fled – free in some terraced house in Earlsdon to say what would have got them killed at home – whilst our English mothers rolled their eyes and reminded them that they didn't need to shout, they weren't in Libya any more.

I was Libyan when we would eat couscous on Sundays, bejewelled with caramelised onions and chickpeas, tomatoey stewed meat and vegetables poured over the top. I was Libyan when my dad would lift us up and shake us whilst my mum hoovered up the small grains of couscous that fell beneath us, which we had inevitably got in between our toes and in our hair (couscous is a messy business when you're a child). I was Libyan when my dad would get a sudden pang of homesickness and grow quiet for the day, looking out the window at our morose English street and imagining he was in the bustle of his home city, where the houses packed tight together like overgrown teeth in a teenager's mouth and lines of washing ran between them like floss. I was Libyan when he'd take out his melancholy on the garage, randomly tidying up the leftovers of our lives into a semblance of order, watching our straight-lipped English neighbours avoid his eye as they slid into their houses and remembering how, at home, everyone knew everyone, how everyone's door was open for a neighbour's child to eat lunch or an old childhood friend to catch up over tea. I was Libyan when that sorrow would metamorphosise into a spontaneous desire to stuff sheep guts with spiced rice and meat, creating *osbaan*, a meal none of us were particularly keen on but that I ate anyway, eager to show him that home could be found here, too.

In the winters, I was English. I would pop a small square of chocolate in my mouth every day in the month of December and count down the days until Christmas. I'd eat roast turkey on the 25th and unwrap my presents in front of the twinkling tree. I was English when I was singing Christmas hymns in school assemblies, my shiny tinsel earrings swinging in time with 'Away in a Manger'. I was English as fireworks exploded in the air and as I made resolutions I'd break within a week. I was English in the rain and in the hail, in the grey din of a British January. I was English when we put on the local radio to listen out for our school listed amongst those closed for snow days. I was English in the spring, as everyone commented on how long the winter was and when warmer evenings suddenly felt full of hope. I was English writing Valentine's cards to my friends and making nests for Easter chicks. I was English as the days got longer and our school trousers turned to checked summer dresses, as we laced together daisy chains and watched aeroplanes trace lines across the sky.

Then, suddenly, I was Libyan again, usually around the end of July. I don't know exactly when it would happen, when and where the parts of me would do their silent exchange. *She's yours for the summer. See you again in September.* Perhaps it was the last day of school, when I'd go home to the house turned upside down as we packed our lives into suitcases for the next six weeks. Maybe it was the first day of the summer holidays, when my parents, my younger brother and I would head out on the two-hour drive to Heathrow Airport. Inevitably running late and having forgotten something, we would rush down the motorway at breakneck speed, my dad's driving getting increasingly erratic as the clock ticked closer to departure time, my mum berating him with her eyes. 'We're not in Libya yet!' she'd tease, transporting us all to the lawless roads of Benghazi and the incessant beeping that sounded in every corner of the city, as constant and pervasive as birdsong. Or maybe it was in Heathrow itself, as I'd puke my guts out due to travel anxiety in the toilets whilst my parents solemnly watched the clock. It could be when we were on the rickety Libyan Arab Airlines plane, halfway across the ocean with England behind me and Libya on the horizon. Or as we landed, when the plane erupted in applause or when the hot gush of desert air smacked us in the face as we climbed down the stairs to the tarmac.

Either way, for the next month and a half, there was no balancing act. I'd eat with my hands, stay up too late and drink more Pepsi (Bebzi) than I'd ever be allowed at home. I'd sleep at a different auntie's house every night, eat shawarmas and knock-off Nutella straight from the jar at 3 a.m. I watched horror movies on MBC and sang along to songs I didn't understand the lyrics to. Everyone fasted until sunset and we broke our fasts on dates and milk as the mosques around the city reverberated with the word of God. We sat on the kitchen floor peeling almonds, stuffing courgettes, squeezing the juice out of tomatoes and chopping onions. Picking grapes straight from the vine and olives straight from the tree, we'd deliver them to neighbours armed with stock phrases I memorised beforehand. We'd float weightless in the hot salt bath of the Mediterranean Sea as the sun roasted our skin. Listening to the sounds of faraway crickets and the whoosh of ceaseless traffic, I'd dip freshly made bread in saccharine mint tea as my aunties gossiped about somebody's son and somebody's daughter.

Then, again, as abrupt as it had arrived at the helm of summer, the exchange would occur again. A plane would land on the grey London tarmac, serenaded by the familiar pitter-patter of rain, and we'd dig out the hoodies we had packed in our backpacks that we hadn't needed for the best part of two months. The muted, brusque, clinical sound of the English language being spoken around me for the first time in six weeks would remind me that I was English again. At least, for now.

At first I thought it was a flaw in my character to slice myself up into separate parts. Other people didn't struggle to see their mixed-race identities in such conflicted, tumultuous ways. Such people seemed to view it as the best of both worlds, whereas I felt marooned between two. Why was I overcomplicating it? But now I realise that this is a primary function of whiteness itself. Whiteness isn't designed to be diluted; it cannot exist alongside anything else. In order for whiteness to be the preserve of privilege and power, it means that necessarily it must become tainted as soon as it is mixed with anything else. Whiteness with a drop of *anything* is no longer truly white. There is no such thing as being part white. I might be half English, my genealogy might be 50 per cent Anglo-Saxon, but the reality is that the brown in me negates the white. I never was and never will be half *white*, just like a person can never be half privileged, half powerful, half immune to the violence of the state. Half free from structural racism.

We have words for it these days. Terms that can explain away that feeling of being two halves instead of a whole. We call it code-switching. So rational, so detached a word to describe lacerating yourself into parts and deciding which is the most palatable for which audience, which *you* is acceptable for this context. Code-switching is often construed as empowering – getting ahead of the current, learning to navigate structural prejudices, to take charge of your othering. But code-switching itself confirms that we must live our lives by codes, by rules, by standards and by norms. That we must conform fully at any one time. We have no language for being more than one thing at once. We only know and we are only taught how to switch, to slot ourselves in, to constantly, constantly please.

Now, I can look back at my childhood and see that I wasn't ever really one thing or another at any given point. I was perpetually a half thing – not quite complete. It's little wonder I was hit with a midlife-crisis level of introspection before I was barely through puberty. They may have been only glimpses, but the *other* me was always there whilst I inhabited whichever version my environment called for. My foreignness was a spectre in the distance that emerged as I was eating dinner with my white grandparents, growing closer as they pointedly served us chicken whilst they ate pork and made comments about it being such a shame we can't have a bite of sausage. It was there when people overcomplicated my straightforward name and asked me where I was really – no, *really* – from. It grew larger when I'd have to explain that I couldn't sleep over at my friends' houses for the fiftieth time because it was 'against my dad's religion' (which I had presumed it must be, down to the steadfastness with which my parents stuck to this rule). It was there, it was always there, forming a ball of alienation and confusion in the depths of my stomach.

The opposite was true, too. My whiteness lingered threateningly in the periphery as I struggled to converse with my Libyan cousins; my fumbled, stunted Arabic a reminder that I wasn't a *proper* Libyan and my strange English habits outing me as unavoidably *different* there, too. I gave everything to fitting in every summer when we went to Libya. I'd hate it when my cousins wanted to practise their English on me or refer to me as their English cousin to their friends. I was jealous of how utterly at ease with their Libyanness they were. How they knew the nuances of language, culture and habit that only a native can pick up. I was embarrassed of my ungainly, uncontainable Englishness – the way I pronounced certain words and how I didn't know the right thing to say at the right time or know how to eat *aseeda* (a giant mound of dough covered in date molasses) with my hands or suck the bone marrow out of a piece of meat. Even now, as an adult, I am ashamed of how I have to rehearse a conversation with my dad before wishing a cousin congratulations on their engagement, how I don't innately know the right phrase to say when someone has passed away, how after the birth of my son, my aunties showered me with the most intricate, eloquent blessings and wishes and all I could muster was *shukran, shukran. Thank you, thank you.*

I talk a lot about how my visible Muslimness is what ejected me from whiteness, but in truth, a nation like Britain pounces on any semblance of weakness as soon as it can sniff it out, othering and segregating long before our adult selves are aware of what is befalling us. The veneer of whiteness soon shatters for those who don't rightfully deserve it, for those who don't truly succumb to its regimented demands. It was already dwindling when I was a non-white toddler in the arms of my clearly white mother and people looked at her with judgement. It was bursting at its seams when I explained to the dinner ladies at school that I couldn't eat pork because my dad was Libyan (that's what I thought the reason was) and they looked at me like I had just calmly informed them that I was an alien. Whiteness was long gone by the time my friends were sneaking sips of decades-old alcohol taken from the back of the kitchen cupboard and calling me boring for faking a stomach ache to go home. Even when I thought I belonged, I didn't. Even when I held whiteness in my hand, it was already slipping through the cracks of my fingers.

Like all children do, I learned how to be a person through watching my parents. Except my personhood was separated into two people who represented each half of me. When I consider how I came to think of my identity later on, I realise it's no coincidence that my parents viewed each other's homelands with derision and even scorn. My mum had lived in Libya for five years before I was born and made it clear she wasn't willing to repeat that experience in a hurry. My dad had grown resentful from decades of languishing in England when his heart yearned to return home, which he would have done long ago if it wasn't for his now-British family keeping him here. Despite their union having created me, I never saw a way that Englishness and Libyanness could exist in harmony – and certainly not within me – because my parents seemed bound together only in spite of their divergent backgrounds and never because of them.

This book explores much of the *after* – how the hijab changed everything for me and what happened to my sense of self after being well and truly otherised for good. But for there to be an after, there must be a before, and that was as fiercely personal as it was political.

Growing up, I was a daddy's girl and by that I mean that I have always felt the pangs of my father's heart twinned in perfect sync with my own. From childhood, I could interpret the frown lines and understand the sighs. I saw the crumpled wax-paper hands from the hours of manual labour and could read in them the sacrifice and the silent, swallowed pain. I knew, innately, that as the firstborn child, my birth had changed the course of my parents' lives, that my dad was here in this country he loathed because of – and for – me. I felt not obliged but compelled to show him that glimmers of home could be found here, too, knowing it would cheer him up if I paid special attention in one of his impromptu Arabic lessons at the dining table or stayed to speak to whichever relative he was on the phone to when everyone else invented an urgent reason to leave the room.

At the same time, I was a pre-teen who clashed with her mother like every girl has in the history of the universe. I was painfully aware that I wasn't like her, that I wasn't going to inhabit the same spheres of womanhood that she dwelled in. I was chubby and she was thin, she was white and I was… something else, whatever that was. She fulfilled society's standards of what it means to be white, to be a woman, and I already knew I didn't. My fierce love for her as my mother collided with a secret hidden anger: I almost blamed her, inexplicably, because it was her womb that had spawned this two-sided existence that didn't make sense to me. I envied her for being so sure about who she was when I couldn't find that out myself and for having grown up without the weight of racism weighing down upon her. I imagined her as the homely Libyan mother that my aunties were, who spent their days making pasta from scratch and cleaning the bathrooms, dishing up extravagant dishes three times a day and most of all passing on genes to their children that make them one thing rather than two.

I associated my mother with my Englishness and with my whiteness because, after all, it came from her. And so, the more I was socially and politically maligned by the racism I was increasingly experiencing, the more distant I felt from the woman who had saddled me with this hotchpotch identity to begin with. I felt bitter, as though it would have been easier if I didn't have any whiteness in me to try to belong to in the first place. Likewise, the more I was racialised in public and the more I was outcasted from the white spaces I had once inhabited with ease, the more I began to identify with my dad and with his culture, even if that wasn't the sum of all my parts. As the Arab Spring dawned, this became a vehicle into my Libyanness that I had never been given before. I may not have understood all the social cues and nuances of language as a 'real' Libyan, but I *could* become an expert on the politics and, ironically, my free access to social media in the west meant that I could know even more than my family on the ground. I became obsessed with the Arab Spring and the subsequent political conflicts in Libya. I pinned Libya's new freedom flag to my school uniform and spent my lunchtimes on Twitter following every latest development. I shared so much, and with such detail and urgency, on my newly created Twitter account that I even had western journalists contacting me for interview because they thought I was a rebel fighter on the front lines and not a schoolgirl from the Midlands. But like all politics, it was fleeting. Gaddafi was overthrown and Libya descended into a power vacuum and was plunged into civil war, and my GCSEs came and went and I no longer knew everything that was happening. The instability in the country, as well as a spate of kidnapping of foreign nationals, meant that my dad no longer thought it was safe for us to visit, and then all at once my summers were no longer spent in a place where the air thickened like treacle but in the solemn malaise of England. And then, again, Libyanness, like Englishness, was a part of my identity that may have been bound to my DNA but felt further away than ever.

Whilst the geographical core of my whiteness was here in the UK, much of what I was latently learning about whiteness came from my time in Libya. Privilege, after all, manifests as a blindfold to those it is endowed upon. Like many formerly colonised lands, Libyan society is obsessed with light skin. Women wear gloves so their hands don't turn brown whilst driving. Teenage girls avoid the sun at midday lest their skin become anything but milky. Women with the whitest skin have the best prospects, the best chance of marrying into a reputable family. Bleaching creams are applied daily like moisturiser. A white-skinned woman at a wedding will find herself flogged by multiple mothers of eligible bachelors who already see visions of their future white grandchildren reflected in her complexion.

I remember laying down to sleep next to my cousins one night – the way we always did, on *fraash* mattresses spread out on the floor in my auntie's sprawling *marbo'a* (a room built for guests). We'd been to a wedding and we traced the henna on our hands, hummed the songs whose volume still pounded in our chests and dreamed of ourselves as brides. My youngest cousin turned to me and said, 'You're lucky, you'll be able to marry a nice man,' and when I asked 'Why?' she said, 'Because you're white.'

'I'll get someone old or mean,' she added. We were eleven.

The funny thing is, I didn't think I was white. Skin-tone-wise, I was at my darkest, having baked in the hot Mediterranean sun for the past six weeks. Identity-wise, I knew I wasn't white either. I had watched enough eyes dart between my grandparents and this brown-ish child inexplicably calling them Nanny and Grandad to know that people didn't see us as the same.

What my cousin had meant, of course, was that I had more proximity to whiteness and by default more access to the privilege it promises. I couldn't see it at the time, but the way my aunties always berated me for letting myself get so brown in the sun, how some of my cousins delighted that they were now whiter than me – even how they said that I should have got my mother's blue eyes instead of my brother (as though I had a choice in the matter) – was because they saw whiteness for what it was. It is something that can be given or denied, something that must be earned and maintained. Something delicate and ephemeral, something ravenous for constant upkeep, something that can be lost in an instant if it isn't preserved. Like milk, something that curdles as soon as anything else infiltrates it. Something that goes bad in the sun.

CHAPTER 2

BLOOD, BONE AND CHIFFON

HOW THE HIJAB CHANGED EVERYTHING

The glint in his eye tells me he pledged his allegiance to defending the borders of Great Britain roughly around the same time he exited the womb.

He informs me that I have been selected for random additional screening, gesturing in wild circles around my head to indicate that the cause for this absolutely random screening is the shiny blue hijab I'm wearing.

'Take a step to the side for me, please.' Curtness reveals the spiky edges of his voice.

Up to this point in my fourteen years of life, I had regarded people in authority as trustworthy, with noble and caring intentions, if a little pernickety about rules like finishing your homework and going to bed on time. But this was different. For the first time, I was being perceived as a threat – a thing to be handled with suspicion and derision. Inside, I felt wrong: a hot sensation of shame and self-contempt. The beeping and clattering, talking and whirring of the people and the airport machinery around me grew jaded, as it was drowned out by the fierce gush of my own pulse in my ears.

I wait by the side as instructed and I lock eyes with my younger brother who has already passed through the metal detector entirely uneventfully, without so much as a second glance from anyone. He raises his eyebrows and I shrug in reply. I'm glad we are too far apart to speak. How do I convey what is happening, this thing morphing between us that I cannot name?

I am taken to a small windowless room where a woman sizes me up with beady, excessively lined eyes. There's another detector, this time an entire booth, and she explains that I'll have to stand in it whilst it X-rays me. I picture cameras burrowing down to the marrow of my bones, checking if there's a suspicious package concealed in my platelets.

'Please remove the head dress, love.'

It takes me a moment to realise what she means by 'head dress'.

I set about unwrapping my scarf, which is no easy feat given that barely a fortnight into wearing the hijab, I am still at the stage of relying on no fewer than ten pins and a whole lot of luck to keep it in place. She watches my quivering hands search for the exact location of each pin, a bemused smirk curling her dry lips at the edges.

After what feels like a year, I've managed to unwrap one layer. 'Nearly there,' I reassure her, with a nervous and hollow laugh. She purses her lips and asks to see my passport. Taking a seat, she throws her legs ostentatiously onto a small plastic table, folding one over the other, browsing my passport like it's this morning's tabloid paper.

'Nay-deen,' she starts, mispronouncing my name as most people do. 'Ash… as… az… barley?'

Naydeen Azbarley – easy first name, confusing surname. Half familiar, half foreign. My oxymoronic identity summed up within my name itself.

'Where you coming from, then?'

'Benghazi… uh, Libya.'

'Lebanon?' she says.

'Umm, no, Libya.'

She regards me as though I informed her I'd just returned from a colony on the moon.

'My dad's from there,' I explain.

She looks at my passport and back to me again, taking in the stark difference between the child in the photo and the slightly older child in front of her who looks decidedly more foreign.

Finally having unwrapped my scarf, she signals for me

to turn around in a circle like some sort of bleak fashion show as she inspects my scalp, pulling my bun side to side, up and down.

'How come you bother with that, then?' she asks, ushering me into the 3D scanner.

'Well,' I begin, before realising that I don't quite know what to say. Nobody has yet asked me that question.

When I think back to this encounter at the airport, I realise that something significant and concrete occurred in that moment. A shift – in me, in my family, in how we define ourselves and how we are perceived in the eyes of others. When my brother and I, who share the exact same set of parents, were separated – him going through security without so much as a second glance, and me, set aside for questioning, for scrutiny – I realise that what I am witnessing is the making of who I am and the breaking of who I was.

They may not have realised it, but these border staff made a decision in that moment that would define me for life. Or maybe that was what they intended to do all along.

That's the thing about airports. Peel back the shiny veneer and you will find the state and its multi-tentacled, violent core reproduced in miniature, hiding beneath the heady delights of duty free and 10 a.m. burgers. Masquerading amongst the excitement and the travel anxiety, the emotional farewells and intimate reunions, is the thrumming brutality of surveillance, racialisation and subjugation.

I didn't know it before, but when I landed in Heathrow wearing the hijab on British soil for the first time, I was discovering something about how my home country – my friends, family, future employers, agents of the state and strangers in the street – would come to see me. When I was kept aside, made to remove my hijab with a camera prodding through layers of my body as though it was my very being that was a threat, this wasn't simply a busybody with a badge and a metal detector making my life difficult. It was the British state serving me notice of my foreignness, my otherness. My eviction from its embrace.

Everything I thought I knew about my identity – my ability to compartmentalise the facets of myself, to fold them all up inside of me and be in control of which one to inhabit in which place and in which instant – was shattered.

Satisfied there's nothing explosive hidden in my organs, the lady allows me to go. I re-wrap my hijab the best I can without a mirror, and I'm let out of the small oppressive room to reunite with my brother. As she hands me back my passport, she says, 'You know, you don't need to wear that here,' as though she expects me to drop to the floor in intense gratitude for her permission. That's when I realised this country had a dress code and I'd just flouted it.

My brother and I walk through 'nothing to declare', and I wonder if I do now have something to declare. Not the dates and dried meats lovingly packed by my auntie Aziza amongst our T-shirts and socks, but maybe my very existence needed laying out on the pop-up table to be inspected before being allowed into society, my DNA scrutinised for signs of foreign threat.

Eventually, we are reunited with our parents, who we haven't seen for a month. Thanks to the incredibly laggy Yahoo! Messenger on my uncle's bulky computer, they already know that I have started to wear the hijab. Knowing my teenage self, I had probably said something like 'started wearing hijab lol' before the internet cut out and I went back to watching MBC4 horror movies with my cousins, oblivious to the weight of my revelation. This was the first time they were going to see me as a hijabi. But they were my parents. I wasn't worried.

Naively, I didn't think it would be any more significant than them seeing me with a tan, a new haircut or a particularly vibrant jumper.

It was just a split second, but it was long enough for me to see.

In my dad's eyes, I saw racist violence in the shadow of Thatcher's broken Britain. I saw skinheads and police batons hunting brown skin. The letters 'NF' graffitied on brick. Landlords slamming doors and stomachs twisting with hunger, young hands grown old with manual labour. I saw broken dreams glinting darkly like shattered glass and I saw fear – fear for what he knew this country was capable of, replicated towards his little girl.

And then I looked at my mum and I saw a woman who didn't recognise the child she had given birth to, and I witnessed a gulf open up between us, right there on the marbled floor of Heathrow. It scared me, this chasm that tore us apart, and I took that look in my mum's eye and swallowed it, letting it sit like sediment in my stomach.

In that moment suspended in time before we all embraced and rushed back to the car before the ticket ran out, I saw what had always been true: that my parents were not one entity but the two halves of me projected before my eyes; two directions to take my life; two versions of my future. And I knew that with the rustle of the shiny blue fabric around my head as I approached them, I had chosen my side.

I have always said that a piece of cloth on my head doesn't define me. In fact, those very words probably made their way into at least one Facebook status of my teenage years. I would have worn them on an edgy T-shirt if such a thing existed. But it's a lie. My hijab has come to shape everything about me – how I am perceived by others and even how I see myself. It negates my biology, eclipses my upbringing and supersedes all other aspects of my identity. At times, it feels like I'm made of chiffon and jersey, metal pins and social expectation instead of flesh and bone.

When, at the age of fourteen, I chose to start wearing the hijab, I was doing much more than my younger self realised or even understood. I like to think it was empowering, this decision that forever altered the fabric of my life, destroying relationships and redirecting the trajectory of my future, but it was more like constructing a giant target and sticking it permanently to my back. A target that I still wear now, a decade and a half later.

Ironically, my decision to wear the hijab was remarkably easy. Almost too easy. It was everything that came before and everything that transpired afterwards that was cripplingly hard.

It was the morning after we had been to the beach and my cousins and I lay our sun-heavy bodies on thin *fraash* mattresses on one of their bedroom floors. Our skin still tingled like the touched endings of a nerve as the AC blew cold air over our sleeping forms, limbs dense with the salt of the sea, skin tender and glistening like we had captured the gold of the sun in our pores. Maybe it was the semblance of belonging so fully, so absolutely, amongst my aunties' daughters that silently pushed me to such a momentous decision, but I woke up that early afternoon and told my cousin, whose room I was staying in, that I wanted to wear the hijab. A statement so insignificant, so easy, that it blinded the years of ache and longing, rejection and humiliation that would come after. She nodded and unlatched the window slats in her room, dousing us in syrupy light. Silently, she opened her drawer, pulled out a soft purple scarf and showed me how to wrap it.

'Helwa,' she smiled. *Sweet.* 'It suits you. Keep it.'

Later, we went to 20th Street: the place where cigarette smoke and exhaust fumes pool in the sky and halogen shop signs spill light onto the black pavement whilst the hungry eyes of bored teenage boys glimmer in the moonlight. My cousins and I bustled into rows of hijab shops and we giggled as we tried on garish prints and outlandish colours, tying extravagant bows under our chins like sophisticated elderly ladies. I spent my Eid money on four different scarves, including a black one for school, and the shop owners gave me little paper booklets containing Qur'anic verses when they heard my broken Arabic. Then, we piled into my cousin's car and ate shawarmas whilst our elbows dug into each other's ribcages, licking the hot, fragrant oil dripping down our wrists.

At first, it was novel. Amusing. I was play-acting an identity I didn't quite know I had permission to inhabit, like the forbidden thrill of trying on your mum's high heels for the first time. I was congratulated everywhere I went by aunties, uncles, cousins and neighbours who were pleased, if a little surprised, by my sudden decision.

In truth, I didn't think about the hijab for the next couple of weeks beyond trying to learn how to wrap it myself without the assistance of at least three cousins armed with pins and contradictory advice. I had stepped on a massive, devastating grenade and I was yet to feel the blow: the adversity had been delayed by the shield of protection I had around me in Libya, where almost every woman wore the hijab and nobody considered their covered bodies a threat.

I never for a second imagined that a piece of material on my head would change so much.

It is no exaggeration to say that everything warped and twisted the moment I stepped foot in England wearing the hijab. It entirely altered the way I was viewed in the eyes of others and, eventually, in my own, too. It changed how non-Muslims and Muslims alike saw me. I've now come to think of my life as pre- and post-hijab. The before and the after.

I went from being invisible and inconspicuous – a child doing normal things like going to school, riding her bike and being reluctantly dragged around Tesco by her mum – to being watched, judged, assessed wherever I was.

The first day I wore it at school, a girl I barely knew in my year told me she could no longer look at me the same way. My favourite teacher, who taught us French and German and who considered me her star pupil (because I was the only one who didn't fall asleep or heckle her in lessons), called me 'Rukshana' for the whole first lesson – the name of the only other visibly Muslim girl in our class. If I needed proof that people weren't going to bother to see the face beyond the swathes of fabric, I'd just been served it on a massive, unmissable platter.

Everywhere I looked, I was being sized up; the categories

that people had put me in were shifting all around me. Humiliatingly, even the few Muslim girls at school (who I had been secretly and desperately hoping would sweep me into their embrace) thought I was pulling a prank, a white girl dressing as a Muslim for a dare.

Whilst the reaction at school was suffocating and denigrating, the verdict of strangers was downright hostile and frightening. One day my best friend and I were crossing a road in her affluent, predominantly white area and a car slowed down and shouted, 'Go home!' I think about this incident now with a great shadow of irony eclipsing the pain and shame that I felt in the moment because, funnily enough, my friend and I were both half-English. Except her other half was Scandinavian and I had the gall to be half Libyan. Tainted with brown. And as we stood there, two teenagers in our own hometown, both as biologically English as the other, that jibe was very clearly aimed at only one of us: the visibly Muslim one, the foreign one. I learned then that the way Britain racialises you is shallow and fickle. It does not care about the cold facts of biology. This is not a land where you can dare to appear foreign and expect to come out of it unscathed.

Not long into Year 10, I did work experience at an opticians' surgery with a very white and elderly clientele. I had customer after customer speak to me in that say-English-words-but-shout-them-very-slowly way because they had never considered that a visibly Muslim girl might actually speak English and heaven forbid have been born here. I even had one old man ask me how I was finding living here in England, to which I replied (in my best impression of someone even posher than the Queen) that I found it most pleasant, seeing as I had lived here for fifteen years already.

I had white men gesture shooting me in the Tesco car park and I had white boys call me 'Taliban' on the bus. I had white women tell me that I shouldn't 'dress like that' here in England and I had interviewers for Saturday jobs ask me how my hijab would affect my ability to be a waitress in their cafe – as though I planned to use my hair to serve cups of tea to pensioners. I had security guards follow me around shops and I had strangers complain about 'those foreigners' to my mum and brother whilst they stood right next to me, not realising we were related.

If you grew up in a big, multicultural city, it's perhaps hard to imagine how it feels to be visibly Muslim in a place where people don't look like you. Northampton is significantly more diverse now, but in the mid-2000s, to look outwardly foreign felt fragile and dangerous, like bursting open your ribcage and offering your raw and exposed heart for the taking. Especially in the part of town we lived in. To this day, in my parents' local supermarket, you will find that someone has planted pork products in the small halal section in the freezer. Even when I visit my parents now, I feel eyes on me. The lingering glares and the double takes. The rabid aversion to my audacity to appear visibly Muslim. Going back there now, from my current home in east London, I find myself shocked anew by the racist myopia of my hometown. I see it through my Londoner husband's eyes, who feels like he's stepped into a village from *Midsomer Murders* and expects a racist attack every time we pop up the shops for milk. But my teenage self came to expect it, pre-empt it, absorb it and let it dissipate in the raw acid of her stomach, so it didn't consume her first.

These outside reactions may have been easier to deal with if I had the reinforcement at home to bolster me in the face of external rejection. But, unknowingly, my decision to wear the hijab had sliced our family, our home, in two. This choice of mine which I took so lightly at the time reopened something rotten and hidden at the core of us. I had scratched at a scab I didn't know existed and revealed the pustulating flesh beneath that we'd all been pretending wasn't there.

The way we had navigated our foreignness as a family before this point was to be English with a dab of otherness about us. *No, we don't eat pork and yes, Daddy does do those strange yoga moves on a prayer mat at the end of the day, but we don't need to talk about that. Especially not to others.* And by opting to bundle up my foreignness and display it on my head for everyone to see, I had shattered the happy equilibrium that had been established – this palatable vision of our otherness composed so as to never draw attention to ourselves.

I realise now that my parents' focus was on assimilation: building a stable foundation for my brother and me, giving us a life free of discrimination and disadvantage as they saw it. We had palatably English-sounding names and the most foreign thing about us was that we didn't eat ham sandwiches. Somehow, we understood, without it ever being said, that we were to be English here and Libyan there. That was the way we were to live. I realise now, as an adult, that this was my parents' priority because they didn't have structures of wealth and privilege to fall back on. They didn't have the luxury to experiment with identities when they needed to make sure they could put food on the table for us and keep a roof over our heads. Perhaps between them, a migrant and a daughter of council estates, they knew no other way to be in this nation that demands subjugation to unspoken rules.

But I found that it was only possible to separate yourself so seamlessly, so completely, upon geographic, racial and religious lines if you were just English or just Libyan like each of my parents were. But what if you were both? And what if, as you grew older, the world around you did the racialising for you? What if the other girls in the playground laughed at the black hairs on your legs that weren't golden like theirs? What if other kids said your dad had rabies because he was the only brown face at parents' evening? What if your friends shunned you because you weren't allowed to sleep over at their houses, or your own grandparents treated you with derision because you wouldn't eat the pork sausages that they wanted to make for dinner? What then?

Before I knew it, I was rapidly hurtling towards an identity crisis spurred on by the way the only home country I knew warped around me as I grew older. And now I was daring to stick my head above the parapet and blow apart the sterilised version of our foreignness that we had been taught to inhabit as a family, forcing everyone to question the very foundations we had built our lives upon. The weeks and weeks of stalemate that ensued afterwards – that made me want to revoke my decision altogether – felt like they would never stop. But then they just did. Out of nowhere. And then we never talked about it again – bundling it up in the loft with our broken toys and outgrown clothes.

I don't like to attach so much significance to what is nothing but a cloth on my head, and I am wary of using my voice to talk about something so predictable, so reductive, as though Muslim women are only qualified to talk about head coverings: only interesting when we are mining our subjugation for the public gaze. But I can't help but acknowledge that for me, quite literally overnight, I went from never so much as questioning my right to exist in the place I was born and bred to feeling increasingly rejected, foreign and threatening. The impact of this was that it entirely altered the way I came to see myself and my own racial identity, permanently reshaping my relationship with my whiteness and how I thought I understood my heritage.

I suppose what happened was that without realising it, and without possessing the language to articulate it, I had benefited from white privilege throughout my childhood which was then rescinded indefinitely as soon as I changed my appearance. There are certain manifestations of foreignness that Britain will accept – and some where it draws the line. It embraces brown-skinned Tory Home Secretaries who harbour far-right views and exclusionary, racist politics. Ethnic minority comedians who poke fun at their own race. Muslims who win gold medals and baking contests. Britishness is jealous and possessive. It demands all of you, your loyalty and absolute allegiance. And it is fickle, shallow and materialistic. It wants foreignness to be something private: we must not burden others with our wanton otherness. By wearing the hijab, I had gone against the rules of whiteness itself, had challenged its dominance and infallible superiority. I had held the glimmer of it in my palm and then I rejected it, instead daring to be outwardly foreign in this land that quashes dissent. I had committed the ultimate unforgiveable sin against the state because whiteness, Britishness and everything that the liberal, progressive west holds dear is something we are taught to aspire to, yearn for and idolise. I had committed treason, and you best believe I was punished for it.

Suddenly, the assumption of foreignness followed me everywhere. People asked me where I was from – where I was *really* from. And when I said I was 'half English, half Libyan', it was like I'd never mentioned the English side because now my brownness, my otherness, eclipsed everything.

I am used to it now. After all, this persistence of the state to otherise never ceases. On my university induction day, when we all waited to be issued ID cards, it took me half an hour of queuing to realise that the staff had incorrectly (and without thinking to check) ushered me into the line for international students. On my first day of teacher training, one of the senior teachers kept asking me what foods I used to have at birthday parties as a child, and when I said cheese on cocktail sticks and Mini Rolls, he would not stop pressing until I actually made up foreign-sounding foods that satisfied his ideas of what brown children eat. When I have written articles in which I question an aspect of British culture, such as the money spent on the Queen's platinum jubilee in the middle of a cost-of-living crisis, I have found my inbox flooded with people telling me to go back home, asserting that even if I might be British, my ancestors must have come from somewhere else at some point. In other words, my claim to Britishness is diluted by my half-foreign biology, conditional upon the extent of my patriotism. It's disarming, frightening even, to think that if I had chosen a different trajectory for my life, I could live undetected with the claws of Islamophobia never getting anywhere near me. Like the butterfly effect with a wildly racist conclusion, everything is pinned to that one decision to cover my head one day.

Wearing the hijab forever changed how I came to view my Britishness, my Englishness, my whiteness – whatever I want to call that part of me that had been revoked. It's an uncomfortable truth, but I suppose the shock of no longer inhabiting that plane of white privilege was debilitating, like a rug being pulled from under you that you didn't even realise you had built your entire life upon. I still find myself frozen in this odd, crippling bind with that part of myself, with that side of my identity. Maybe it's a protective mechanism, an act of self-preservation – maybe even defiance – but I've now come to no longer consider myself white. Or English. Or British, in anything but what my passport says.

At first I fought it, my teenage self diligently playing the role of the good Muslim, the cool Muslim, the palatable Muslim. I quickly learned that Muslims are accepted in Britain so long as we are the 'good ones'. Britain requires us to dilute our identities until we become nothing but Muslim in name – and sometimes not even then. Even our names must be repackaged, reduced, bleached of their Muslimness. Mohammeds become Mo. Sameers become

Sam. We must exist within and for the white gaze, poking fun at our otherness, laughing along at terrorist jokes and dressing ourselves in the stereotypes of our own degradation. Every practising Muslim knows the pressure to become the acceptable token – the colleagues pressuring you to come to the pub even if you don't drink ('Well, Bashir comes to the pub even though he doesn't drink, so why can't you?') or to contain your Muslimness so others don't have the inconvenience of seeing it ('Why do you have to wear that? Mariam is a Muslim, but she just dresses like us').

So I smiled politely at the dinner table at my friends' houses when their parents told made-up stories about seeing Arabs trading their daughters for camels when they went to Morocco in 1999, and when my classmates made jokes about me being Osama bin Laden's daughter, I laughed along. When a friend suggested I come to the last day of Year 11 dressed as a terrorist, I pretended to entertain the idea because I didn't yet know to take a step back and examine the weight of these so-called jokes and the cost of my self-mockery. (Incidentally, I was never going to come as a terrorist. I came as a banana. Another story entirely…)

When I needed to pray at my weekend job, I'd pretend to be searching for something in the store cupboard and prostrate with a thumping heart on the cold, dank floor, hitting my head on shelves as I bowed down, hoping that nobody would come in and find me. And if somebody did come in, I'd shoot up suddenly, exclaiming 'found it!' so nobody knew what I was really doing. To my teenage mind, it seemed too foreign, too strange, to be seen praying by these white people who had only just accepted me.

When the manager at that same job said in front of everyone that my hijab made me look like a middle-aged woman, I smiled and let the sniggers and my gaping humiliation become distant white noise whooshing in my ears.

When we'd spend half-term holidays at my grandparents' house and I needed to pray, instead of facing the barrage of questions and jibes about what and how and why I was praying, I'd make an excuse about needing the bathroom and run a tap upstairs whilst I quickly prayed in the next room, barely letting my head touch the ground in case the floorboards creaked. When I had decided to stop eating the non-halal meat that we had grown up on – the Turkey Twizzlers, Chicken Dippers and McChicken sandwiches – I pretended I wasn't hungry any more and pushed my food around my plate, letting the hunger that ravaged my growing form wither inside, because to explain my actions, to betray the idea of our foreignness that they had just about come to accept, felt too terrifying.

I was constantly torn between an innate desire to adhere to the religion I was increasingly finding solace in during my teenage years and feeling exhausted, bitter and frightened at having to explain myself to my closest family and friends. Every Ramadan, my English grandparents would persistently hound us, telling us that it wasn't healthy to fast for eighteen hours straight and weren't we hungry? And not even a sip of water? And don't people die if they don't eat? And are you absolutely sure you're not hungry? And is it your dad making you do this? My brother and I would bat off their questions with one-word answers and cough when our stomachs (inevitably) did rumble so they didn't take it as evidence of our supposed torture.

Every time the temperature rose above ten degrees, I got the same reactions: are you not hot in that? Why do you have to wear that? Can't you wear a T-shirt and shorts? Why did God make your hair if He didn't want you to show it? And the classic: it's such a shame, you had such lovely hair (as though I was now bald). The thing is, of course fasting makes you hungry and covering your body makes you hot, but to admit that felt like succumbing to the idea of Islam as oppressive and cruel, to acquiesce to the idea that whiteness, Englishness, was superior. And the alternative – to explain my actions, why I wanted to fast, why I wanted to wear the hijab, to articulate the befores and the afters, the wheres and the whys to people who had known me my whole life and who had invested in this idea of me being just like them – just felt so crushing and daunting that I simply couldn't manage it. So at barely fifteen, I mastered the art of concealing my feelings, my beliefs and the parts of me that didn't align with how everyone else wanted to see me.

And so when I was at my friend's house and they suggested they stage pictures in which they pretended to beat me up whilst I was praying, pulling on my clothes and pretending to kick me as I bowed down, I let them. I laughed an empty laugh along with them and cloaked my shame in the reassuring façade of assimilation and acceptance. And then when I saw those pictures uploaded onto Facebook for hundreds of people to see, with random uncles, family friends and neighbours'-sisters'-dogs'-cousins 'lmao'-ing at these images, I took that bubbling humiliation and the rising tide of doubt knocking at my ribcage and I locked it away somewhere I couldn't find it.

But it didn't work. Because not even offering up your dignity on a plate is enough to placate the insatiable appetite of the British state to racialise, categorise and subjugate. So what if my friends thought I was an acceptable kind of Muslim, if that white man on the bus still whispered 'Paki' to me? So what if my grandparents saw me as passably English, if my teachers still asked me if I was going to have an arranged marriage? It didn't matter that my name sounded English and I'd grown up on baked beans and potato smileys, because when my friends started smuggling boys into their rooms and sneaking into clubs, I was just the awkward foreign appendage to the group who didn't do the things that were deemed cool. And I was that granddaughter who now wears long sleeves in the height of summer and sticks out like a sore thumb in their small white village. I had become an expert at filing down the jagged edges of my Muslimness and yet that still wasn't enough. It would never be enough.

Refusing to be that 'good Muslim' is a radical act, and it's one I wish I had learned to do sooner. You cannot trick a nation state as intent on forced assimilation as Britain into accepting you in your true unapologetic form. No matter how much I tried to deny it to myself, to cling on to that waning mirage of belonging, I was already racialised and categorised wherever I went, and eventually the microaggressions, jibes, stereotypes and misconceptions wore me down to the point where I came to see myself as an outsider entirely, giving up the idea that I belonged.

Instead, I revoked my own Britishness, my own whiteness, because those who seemed to have a greater claim to it had shunned me – so who was I to continue to consider myself English, British, white? I became increasingly uncomfortable in white spaces that I had once occupied with ease, and desperately sought out situations where I would no longer be the only minority. I clung on to my brownness, embraced my otherness and found solace in the faith that had always been a mere backdrop to my childhood. I searched for ways to appear even more visibly Muslim, ditching jeans for abayas, getting my nose pierced (to my teenage mind, this cemented my Brown Girl Status) and spending hours every night watching the few grainy hijab tutorials that could be found on YouTube back in the late 2000s, basking in the sheer power to make myself look so different with a simple twist of fabric or placement of a pin. I trawled Yahoo! Answers, learning things about my religion that I had never known before. I did the unthinkable and moved cliques at an all-girls' school, gravitating towards the corner of the canteen that the student body (appallingly) referred to as 'Asia'. I entered into friendships that didn't require me to shapeshift, becoming soul sisters with girls who could know every part of me. We prayed together in our head teacher's small office at lunchtimes, and we called each other's parents auntie and uncle when we spent Saturdays at each other's houses. We were different races, cultures and classes, but we were united in our status of otherness, unified in our Muslimness; we found a home together as our peers seemed to grow into their burgeoning whiteness all around us. For the first time, I felt like I could be myself.

At the same time, it was like my eyes had been fine-tuned to the nature of this country I called home, and through its rejection of me, I became more aware of its inherent and entrenched imperfections, the way it cements the subjugation of the other.

I saw myself at primary school age, rummaging through bathroom drawers with the hot welt of my tears stuck in the base of my throat, finding an old forgotten razor and taking the crusty, rusted blade to my leg. I saw the crimson shock of my blood dripping into the bathtub and my mum asking me what on earth I had done. I saw the faces of the girls who had pulled up my trouser legs at school, laughing at the hairs underneath. I thought about how that prank had followed me to secondary school with an entirely different set of friends, how that was part of my slow, hidden racialisation. It felt a sinister and disturbing revelation: I hadn't always been as immune to the assault of whiteness as I thought.

I saw myself and my brother as children, with his lighter skin, blue eyes and mousy hair. And I saw the pall of pity on people's faces as they said, 'It's a shame she didn't get her mother's eyes,' or even when my aunties in Libya warned me to stay out of the sun because my skin had the tendency to turn brown under its strong Mediterranean rays – and somehow, inherently, I knew that meant my worth would be depleted. I realised that my whiteness had only ever been conditional and transient, a trick of the light. The veneer was shattering and the result was both gutting and inflaming, rousing a defiance within me to reject my whiteness in all its facets and cling to my brownness, my religion and anti-racist politics.

In writing this, I've had to think deeply about why this period of my life, after I had chosen to wear the hijab, was so difficult and why it shaped my adult choices so much. If I hadn't faced such an acute rejection from everything and everyone I knew, would I have gone on to seek out the safe spaces that allowed me to meet the people that lay the foundation of my life today?

Without these experiences, would I be a practising Muslim? Am I actually just secretly, somewhere deep inside, somehow resentful that I am no longer able to inhabit that position of whiteness that I once did? And does this exploration of my identity come across as me simply being desperate to be white?

As an adult, I've gone on to live and teach in places like east London with hugely diverse populations, and I'm always blown away by how teenagers here are so brazenly, unapologetically British along with their Muslimness. That's not to say they adhere to rigid notions of what Britishness is, but rather that they refuse to be maligned – they never consider themselves anything but British, because why should they? I find myself almost jealous of the breezy nonchalance with which my students reply 'London' when they're asked where they're from – meanwhile I find myself doing mental mathematical equations whilst sweating profusely when met with the same question.

But I've come to realise that the reason I found the dismantling of my whiteness so painful is that as a child I was under the naive notion that identity was something inherited and irrefutable.

My fairly 'English' childhood furnished me with the incorrect belief that I had a non-negotiable claim to Englishness – even if I was only *half*. As a child, I didn't realise how much of what I saw around me was the result of race – our class, my dad's job, my parents' marriage, my grandparents' suspicion of my dad, why we spent every summer in Libya. I didn't understand that this was all predicated on my dad's experience with being racialised in this country and what that meant for the rest of us. I was sheltered by the familiar cloak of fish and chips, fizzy pop and half terms spent riding bikes in white villages with white grandparents. I wasn't prepared for what my teenage and adult selves would have to face, because I was being brought up by a mother who had never had to experience such a thing and a father who never expected to face anything but. I didn't know that my claim to whiteness was only temporary – revocable as soon as I dared to stray from it. And now I realise that the reason that felt so difficult for me is because sometimes it's easier to have never had something in the first place than to have it taken away from you. My whiteness was a coal that eventually became too hot to hold, and it's only when I stepped away from it to see my calloused hands that I realised it had been burning me the whole time.

I'm not resentful that I can no longer inhabit white spaces without feeling uncomfortable or actively discriminated against, because I no longer wish to enter those spaces. But I suppose a part of me will always be angry that

that choice was taken away from me so suddenly and viciously by people whose Englishness is only as valid as my own, and that Britishness is so utterly unwavering that it cannot bend to accept those who don't conform to its parochial ideals. Sometimes, when I face racism – particularly when people assert that I don't *really* belong here – I feel tempted to whip out a picture of my mum and let her Anglo-Saxon features baffle my opponent like some kind of supreme trump card. I consider fashioning a quick family tree to prove that, in fact, half of my heritage is only about as exotic as Scotland and Ireland. That I, too, have relatives who read the *Daily Mail* (sadly). But that just proves the point of racists, of white supremacy, of this flimsy notion of whiteness itself. If I was to be deemed English enough by some racist on the bus because of my mum's blue eyes or affinity to Marmite and *Corrie*, that surely means that I am just cementing the idea that people who have no hint of whiteness in their genealogy deserve to be the victims of systemic prejudice, even if I don't? It's a zero-sum game and harms only the already structurally disadvantaged: people who are racialised the same as I am anyway.

Yet still, even with my hijab, I cannot deny that I still benefit from much of the white privilege of my childhood through my passably English-sounding first name, my accent and my British upbringing and education. Those living in poverty, grappling with their immigration status or facing the concurrent discriminations of anti-blackness and Islamophobia don't have the same privileges I have, even if I feel that my own have been depleted. So I have reached a stage where my whiteness becomes a moot point; it's gone full circle – it was ripped from under me and now I cannot – and will not – embrace it without throwing others to the wolves. It feels now like a rapidly disappearing figure in the rear-view mirror of my past – something that I am not even sure was ever there to begin with.

CHAPTER 3

CENTRAL RESERVATIONS

THE DICHOTOMY FACING MUSLIM WOMEN

You're standing in the central reservation in the middle of a motorway. The speed limit is 70 mph, but everyone is going at least 100, feet slammed down on pedals so hard that ligaments protrude from skin, veins pulse in temples and exhaust fumes spike the air.

Hurtling in opposite directions are ten-tonne trucks and articulated lorries that shudder and groan like metal monsters. They speed past so fast that you can feel the sound shake your ribcage, rattle in your bones, churning the marrow inside, so close you swear you can feel the hair on your arms brush their exterior.

You are absolutely, entirely, still. Fear freezes even your eyeballs. Unable to move, the mere rise and fall of your chest feels like an invitation for death. The slightest involuntary movement, a stray hair in the breeze or the twitch of your nose, and you'll be dragged by the force of the oncoming traffic, skull smacking into the tarmac of the road.

So what do you do? You make yourself still.

Silent.

Small.

You cower, crouch down with your hands over your head, and you close your eyes and you wait until, if ever, it finally ends.

This is how it feels to be a Muslim woman in a nation like Britain.

It is to exist at the intersection of violent misogyny and gendered Islamophobia, neo-colonial feminism and culturally ingrained patriarchy. It is to attempt survival with all these factors tugging at you. To forge a life when everything you say, wear and do is potential ammunition for people who hold power over you: your very existence an advert for some myopic ideology or discriminatory policy. It is to be stuck on that central reservation between the opposing lanes of traffic where every step, every movement feels like an invitation for your own destruction. Except the lanes of traffic are contrasting notions and agendas, clashes of the political spectrum. All intent on your downfall. All serving everyone else's interests but your own and proving some outdated, damaging idea about what you are, who you should be or what your existence means. Men in your community and far-right Islamophobes, tutting aunties and patronising feminists, politicians with imperial ambitions and nation states erecting borders. Everyone is vying for our blood.

The mere act of existing as a Muslim woman in Britain feels like assembling a personhood in that liminal space between the noise, the expectation and the danger; to hold on to the inside lip of the in-between, the slice of shade away from the glare of stereotype and categorisation, domination and subjugation.

It is systemic and structural, this entrenched surveillance of our bodies, our beliefs and our actions. The rejected job applications, the lower target grades and the violence of nationalism, citizenship and borders. The statistically higher rates of death in childbirth and the average lower earnings. But it is also the minutiae of the everyday. It is not standing at the edge of the Tube platform because that video of a hijabi being thrown in front of an upcoming train is still etched into the insides of your eyelids. It is walking the long way home to avoid going past the pub in the dark, the one with the St George's flag that wafts like a threat in the breeze above white men clutching pints, stewing in a cloud of hops and nationalistic dreams. It is the lingering stares and the double takes, the pursed lips and the colder reception than the person before you in the queue got. It is answering questions from smug strangers about whether lightning would come and strike you down if you accidentally showed your hair to the postman or ate a bite of a ham sandwich without realising. It is exhausting and all-consuming, designed by the state to wear us down, to control us from the inside.

Violent imperial states with bloody histories of murdering and occupying black and brown bodies have long used the Muslim woman as a symbol of oppression, a justification for brute military force. Colonialism repackaged with a white saviour, feminist twist. After all, surely it's OK to invade a country when it's on the premise of liberating their women from inherently backwards and uniquely misogynistic Muslim men, right? When the French occupied Algeria, they justified their actions on the grounds of defending native women from their 'barbaric' male counterparts. But this concept is not confined to the dusty pages of history books. In 2001, Congresswoman Carolyn Maloney wore an Afghan-style burka whilst giving a speech in the House of Representatives, using her attire to justify the US invasion of Afghanistan. Clearly, the very notion of a woman covered up was supposed to be so utterly contemptible to the collective western imagination that the mere sight of a burka-clad woman in Congress was designed to send the country into a pro-war frenzy. The symbol of the veiled woman is weaponised over and over again to obscure the brutal realities of military occupation, to explain away the inconvenient bloodstains of civilians and corpses of little children.

When I was a teenager, sprawled on my bedroom floor, the Fray playing on LimeWire, painting each nail a different colour and absentmindedly chatting to my friends on MSN, my best friend's boyfriend popped up with a message telling me that he doesn't think anyone should be able to tell me to cover my hair. Now, it wasn't just hormone-fuelled bravado that made this sixteen-year-old boy I hardly knew think he could liberate me with a mere few words and I'd just whip off my scarf, jumping down to his feet in gratitude. It was because we live in a world where Muslim women are perpetually and deliberately presented as entirely devoid of agency at every level – so much so that the mere notion of me choosing to cover my hair was entirely unthinkable, even to a fellow child.

This conceptualisation of Muslim women lays the foundations of not just foreign policy but domestic legislation, too, rendering us mere political footballs to score votes. When David Cameron was Prime Minister, he made a speech insinuating that if only we pesky Muslim women spoke better English, if only we were less 'traditionally submissive', perhaps our children wouldn't be so prone to radicalisation. In fact, despite long clinging to the refrain that there is 'no magic money tree', he even graciously pledged money to help Muslim women learn English (despite having only recently slashed funding for vital local hubs like language classes in community centres, let's not forget).

Here, the image of the backwards, housebound Muslim woman who only understands Urdu, Arabic or Somali and has no knowledge of her child's escapades is weaponised to present us as so primitive and inept that we constitute a national security threat. Forget the material decimation of minority communities already disproportionately affected by poverty that might make a young person disenfranchised with their environment. No, it isn't just that our perceived patriarchal faith is at odds with western democratic ideals of feminism; it renders us dangerous, too – like an inexperienced driver at the wheel of a massive truck on black ice. It is in this way that the Muslim woman is presented, paradoxically, as both victim and threat – meek and malleable yet at once sinister and insidious. Hiding murderous intent in the swathes of our abayas, terrorism in the cadence of domestic chatter in mother tongues.

The British public imagination perceives Muslim women in a strange and reductive contradiction. See us on a make-up billboard in skinny jeans and a turban hijab and we're a symbol of progressiveness. See us in the benefits queue with five children in tow and we're a drain on society, a harbinger of social decline. See us Union-Jack-draped, winning competitions and gold medals and we're the picture of multiculturalism (for as long as we are successful and keep our opinions to ourselves). See us groomed as a child by a terrorist organisation with global power, exploited by older men online in the promise of shiny things like love and glory, and we are made stateless. We are rejected by the country that raised us, our name rendered nothing but a racist jibe and our face plastered over tabloid papers. We become synonymous with evil as our future festers somewhere in a refugee camp on the border of a war-torn land.

This nonsensical duality in how we are perceived as Muslim women is summed up perfectly in the BBC's 2018 political thriller *Bodyguard*. The opening scene features a Muslim woman on a train. She is laden with explosives, putting the lives of everyone on board in imminent danger. It emerges that she is distressed, panicking and desperate, coerced by her terrorist husband to carry the bombs for him. Of course, it falls to the white man to save this poor, meek damsel in a hijab from her evil and primitive Muslim husband. But then, in a twist of events that does precisely nothing to further the cause for Muslim women, it turns out that in fact there is no coercive husband and that she is the terrorist mastermind after all. She simply co-opted the image of the Muslim woman in need of salvation in order to manipulate the authorities and evade punishment. This is hardly an intersectional feminist win. In fact, all it does is reinforce the idea that Muslim women have only two reductive choices, two categories that we are allowed to inhabit in the minds of the British public, on their television screens and in their newspapers. Either we are submissive and subjugated, victims of our own patriarchal cultures and faith – or we are a perverse danger, a veiled threat, wrapping our heads and bodies in our outright rejection of western culture and holding tight to religious views which are at odds with superior, enlightened European values.

The things we watch and read matter. They mould perceptions of the average member of the public and this affects our everyday, lived experience. If we are only ever shown Muslim women who fit very narrow and pre-defined boxes, these stereotypes replicate themselves in our lives, in the form of both microaggressions and immovable systemic barriers. If you live in a big city with a large Muslim population, it is perhaps hard to imagine, but many British people have never met a Muslim and their only understanding of Islam and Muslims is garnered through the tabloid press. Growing up in Northampton in the 2000s, I saw what happens when your entire encyclopaedia of information is from *The Sun* and the *Daily Mail*. From being questioned about Rotherham grooming gangs by a supermarket cashier to finding myself with a captivated, semi-disgusted, audience every time I readjusted my hijab in a public bathroom. Muslim women are a pervasive image in the press, our covered forms hunt the front pages like grim reapers, but we remain an oddity hidden in plain sight because we are never given a platform to dominate our own narratives.

If we were better exposed to portrayals of Muslim women in the things that we watch and read – which usually amounts to little more than pictures of war-torn countries on the 10 p.m. news and derogatory daytime television shows about benefit scammers – perhaps we wouldn't remain such an unknown. Perhaps then stereotypes around us would be harder for the public to swallow and our everyday lives less governed by expectation and prejudice. But be it the state, the public or the way in which Islamophobia seeps into every facet of our lives, there is no appetite for seeing Muslim women as human in a way that doesn't satiate western liberal aims.

As a teacher, I've seen how even children absorb and internalise this perception of Muslim women being something strange and obscure. Take the time I was doing my teacher training in a rural school on the outskirts of the town and my students had never met a visibly Muslim woman before. In the middle of helping one boy decipher the meaning behind a complex metaphor, he turned to me wide-eyed and asked me quite innocently, 'Are you the ones who shoot everyone?' I lost count of the number of lessons that went off in odd trajectories with students asking me things about my faith and the way I dress: questions they'd never had the chance to ask a real-life Muslim before. From delicately worded concerns about how I ended up bald to genuine confusion at how the colour of my hijab changes every day if I can never take it off. More than one student even revealed that they thought I stuck the pins straight into my skull like a pin cushion.

I grew up watching *EastEnders* – or rather sitting at the top of the stairs and watching whilst my mum thought I was asleep. The programme's character Shabnam was the first portrayal of a hijabi I saw on TV. In fact, even when I started to wear the hijab in 2008, it was such a rare occurrence to see another visibly Muslim woman on our screens that at the mere passing glimpse of one, my mum would call me: 'Nadeine, Nadeine! Look, there's a hijabi on TV!' Often, she'd tape a whole episode just to show me a two-second glimpse, and half the time it just ended up being a hood. Or a nun.

As a child, Shabnam was the sole presentation of Muslim women on television. What did she teach a young and impressionable me about what it means to be a visibly Muslim woman in Britain? Well, her character was desperate to remove her hijab and to embark on a double life, seeking freedom in one-night stands in club toilets and secret white boyfriends. The characterisation of Shabnam posited that to be a Muslim woman was something shameful, something to be escaped, something to shed as soon as your parents went to bed like a dirty second skin. Her character reinforced the notion that freedom, progressiveness and liberty are to be found at the bottom of a bottle and only with an uncovered head. What's worse, she cemented in the mind of the British public that Islam is something that binds Muslim women to lives they do not wish to live. We Muslim women are perpetually fed a narrative that salvation lies in us unshackling ourselves from our faith and culture, and growing up exposed to that made a difference to the way I saw my faith and identity, cementing the idea that Muslimness and Britishness cannot coexist.

As I grew older and especially as I became visibly Muslim as a hijabi, I desperately sought out representations of myself around me. My teenage desire to be recognised and seen, to witness all of my frayed edges echoed back at me on a screen or on a page, led me to scour the internet and libraries for anything that made me feel a little less alone, not so alien. I found books that featured hijabi women on the covers, but when I read them, I was left with the same unsettled feeling simmering inside. They taught me that if white boys have a crush on you, you should take your hijab off, or that Muslims were inherently sexist and to be free meant to find solace in the embrace of the west. I spent hours watching illegally downloaded episodes of a Canadian soap opera called *Little Mosque on the Prairie* about a small Muslim community, and I drank up the normality, the monotony of the everyday that it offered me in shapes I could recognise. Instead of being about escaping religion, it was about living unapologetically as yourself. I envied the tiny moving characters that I watched every night; I wanted to jump into my screen and swim in the pixels of their fictional lives, leaving behind the questions of identity, belonging and home that made my own skin feel too heavy to bear.

These days, we see more Muslim women on TV, but things haven't much improved in terms of the representation we are offered. On the news, we are an oppressed and anonymous mass. Our faceless depiction as burka-clad and voiceless is used to justify aggressive military force or enact policies that deepen our subjugation. We are a symbol of a lack of integration, a red flag to the bulls of nationalism and racism.

When we are dramatised, what we see is the archaic, invisible backdrop to a protagonist's search for freedom – the suffocating, traditional home from which they yearn to be free. We are handed mothers dupatta-draped and surgically attached to the oven, harbouring outdated ideas and broken English. We are shown women whose dreams extend about as far as their daughters marrying doctors and reorganising the spice cupboard, interested in nothing but what Shumaila's husband bought her or the price of a baby chicken. We are shown women who hover in the background. Women who suffer at the hands of misogyny: silent and subservient victims of patriarchal codes that are depicted at odds with western ideals. Or women who themselves perpetuate sexism, partaking in honour-based violence towards their wayward daughters or bullying their daughters-in-law. When we are given Muslim women, we are handed characters who are flat, one-dimensional archetypes; symbols of outdated and damaging ideas; undeserving of their own story, their own limelight.

As Muslim women, it is almost impossible for us to exist outside of the white gaze when our entire life remains under its watchful glare. Even in instances where we do see an attempted refreshing take on the Muslim female experience, what we actually get is whiteness repackaged in brown paper, with a hijab stuck on. We get double lives, secret boyfriends and self-hatred. That's not to say that there are not Muslim women, including those who are visibly Muslim, whose lives look like this, but if we are intent on revealing the complex nuances of Muslim womanhood, why is it only the versions that pander to the white gaze that we are shown? We see women taking off their hijab, choosing 'freedom' over faith, but what about the other way round? Women like me who found solace and meaning in the faith that Britain vilifies?

The trope of the Muslim woman is always employed as proof of Islam's – and Muslims' – inherent deficiency. Even when we are allowed into writers' rooms, even when we write literature ourselves, certain narratives are chosen for publication or televisation that simply perpetuate the ideas that already weigh us down. We are rarely ever afforded the subtle, layered humanity that other characters receive. As writer Jack Shaheen puts it, we are either 'billionaires, bombers or belly dancers'.

The media, the public and the state want our stories as long as they fit preconceived narratives. They want to gobble up our subjugation, devour our abusive home lives, our repressed sexual desires, our stories of escaping the confines of our faith, to feast on the fruits of western superiority and become voyeur to our self-caused oppression. To consume our veiled and forbidden flesh.

For me, being a visibly Muslim woman in Britain has meant ridicule and harassment. It has meant attacks from Islamophobes and the faux sympathy of feminists who want to save me. It has even meant rejection from some in my own family. But part of the reason that being a Muslim woman is so utterly draining, so absolutely depleting, is that we cannot even close a metaphorical door and exist at peace within our own communities either. Because for all the hurt and humiliation I have felt at the hands of people on the outside, that is compounded by the way other Muslim women and I have been made to feel by some Muslim men – those on the inside with us.

Whilst I wouldn't think twice about tweeting, ranting or even contacting the police about a racist attack, it would be another matter entirely if it was perpetrated by someone who shares my faith. For many Muslim women, the knowledge of state-entrenched Islamophobia and Islam's reputation as uniquely patriarchal is a chokehold that prevents us from speaking publicly about our subjugation at the hands of Muslim men. To be vocal about how misogyny affects us specifically as Muslim women would risk proving right the people who think Muslims are inherently misogynistic or confirming that our faith is at odds with British values after all – even though all women experience patriarchy in its myriad forms no matter what groups they come from.

But for Muslim women, the weight of the multinational Islamophobia industry which churns out derogatory news and aggressive policy with no end means that when *we* talk about our suffering at the hands of entrenched sexism, we risk heightened state-sanctioned violence towards our entire community and even more exclusionary and nationalistic policy. If we talk about domestic violence, honour killings or female genital mutilation, if we criticise patriarchal cultural norms or the misogynistic misinterpretation of sacred text, not only do we tarnish Islam's already muddied reputation but we also face being accused of airing our dirty laundry in public. So whenever we face oppression at the hands of Muslim men, we must weigh our own suffering and right to justice against these wider implications for our fellow Muslims. And if we do speak out, the potential implications of community-wide harassment still hurt us anyway. So it's a double-edged sword; an impossible quandary that keeps Muslim women silent and allows some Muslim men to perpetuate their subjugation and abuse, on both a systemic and a personal level, protected by the silence that Islamophobia binds us in.

No doubt some will read this and feel relieved, like these words have alleviated them of any blame or responsibility, like I have confirmed that Muslim men were the bad guys all along – like tabloid newspapers and foreign policy have been saying all this time. But, then again, I suppose those people may not be reading this book. Either way, to be safe, I'll add this caveat: my statements about Muslim men do not in any way lessen the blow, the intense and long-lasting suffering, caused by structural Islamophobia. I am not saying that oppression at the hands of far-right racists is any better, and I am certainly not condoning the idea that Muslims are especially and uniquely wired to denigrate women, inherently incapable of perceived western standards of gender equality. But Muslim communities, like all subsets of society, are just as affected by systemic patriarchy as anyone else. Women of all backgrounds face misogyny and are forced to navigate a violently patriarchal world. If I was Sikh, Jewish, Christian or Hindu, I would likely be talking about the way misogyny manifests in my own community, too. Masculine superiority is ingrained in our world – our lives revolve around its throbbing patriarchal core.

That being said, there is something I find undeniably troubling and terrifying about our so-called brothers in faith denying Muslim women our humanity, perpetuating dangerous and violent misogyny and further entrenching us Muslim women in our multifaceted subjugation. Perhaps it's because I expect better from followers of a religion that I believe to be deeply equitable when it comes to gender dynamics. It could be because Muslim men already know how it feels to be harassed at the hands of the state, victims of stereotype and aggressive border policies. Or maybe it's because it means we aren't even safe in our places of worship, our homes, our families.

Ask any Muslim woman who has needed to pray whilst out and she will tell you the same story. The cobweb-filled broom cupboards and the filthy basements. The shacks with no working lights or running water. The grim and the unhygienic, the unsightly and the unsafe. The crevices carved out for us as an afterthought whilst the men pray in lavish halls under chandeliers and calligraphed domes, bowing down onto plush, perfumed rugs.

I have had to pray in the grimy back alleys of mosques, where they've simply added a corrugated tin roof and called it the sisters' section. I've bowed down onto mildew-infested rugs and I've done my wudhu in the middle of a British winter with the outside tap on the back of the building – the only space they've allocated for women to perform their ablutions. In other cities with huge Muslim populations like Birmingham and Leicester, I have been let into women's sections that are pitch black with no working lights and I have prayed in about thirty seconds hoping that the man who let me in doesn't have vile intentions. I have taught in schools that have a designated prayer space for Muslim boys whilst female students pray in the cold playground or at the back of their favourite teachers' classrooms.

Yet, as horrific as these conditions are, it's almost a relief if a mosque does at least have somewhere to pray for women – even if that is a broom cupboard. Much of the time, there is no women's section at all and knocking on a closed door to be met with an uncle who responds to your request as though you have just ordered a rocket to the moon hardly furnishes us Muslim women with the idea that we are an equal and valued part of our community.

Met with no women's space in many mosques, every Muslim woman I know has had to pray in random places like shop changing rooms. Unlike men, we are left to blindly grab an item off the rail and pretend we're going to try it on, often to be met with party anthems blaring and a space barely big enough to bow down without banging our heads or looking like we're peering under the door into the next changing room. Or, when shops are closed, all that's left are the darkened, dirty doorways where we have to put down our jackets to pray in, hoping the noises and shadows behind are just passers-by. I know of Muslim women, braver than I, who have prayed at the back of the men's section if there's no designated space for women. Sometimes they have been left unbothered. Sometimes they have been told to leave, accused of causing a distraction, as though our existence – even when in worship – is something wrong and sinful.

When women try to organise against this, to secure better, cleaner, safer prayer spaces, we are met with backlash from both sides. Muslim men remind us that they have a greater right to prayer space than us, that it is mandatory in Islam for men to pray at the mosque in congregation at specified times but for women it is optional. They twist historic cultural norms that meant women would traditionally tend to be the ones at home with their children to excuse the inequality that we face in our mosques today, ignoring that many women like me feel that access to a mosque is imperative for our spiritual health – especially at isolating times like early motherhood. They deliberately sidestep the reality of modern life where women no longer remain in the domestic sphere to the same extent as the thirteenth century. At the same time, Muslim women are also faced with the two cents of Islamophobes that nobody asked for, who hijack our struggles and use them to prove Islam's deficiency. So what can we do other than keep our qualms to our group chats and our homes, our complaints falling upon the ears of our friends and families – the safe ones – rather than reaching those who can enact material change.

An investigation by the UN in 2021 found that 97 per cent of women in the UK have been sexually harassed. At fourteen, like many girls, I was beginning to realise the endemic of sexual harassment that exists around us, my eyes opening slowly to the way men perceive and consume us as women and girls before we really understand what is happening. From the inappropriate behaviour of male teachers at school to the eyes of men in the street lingering on our checked summer dresses, I look back at my life and, like every woman, I can trace how and where it began by weaving together the instances that made me feel uncomfortable, wrong, blameworthy.

But when I started to wear the hijab, the harassment changed and increased, as though it was a green flag to some Muslim men to sexualise me. Many of my female Muslim friends experienced the same thing as soon as they became visibly Muslim, too – as though our modesty itself was fetishised. This is an uncomfortable thing to talk about publicly, and even as I write this, I am wary of inadvertently reinforcing the orientalist stereotypes of brown men as chauvinistic devourers of women's flesh, who trade women's bodies like cattle, ogling veiled silhouettes on the street corners of sand-covered lands. This stereotype is damaging and unrealistic. But the reality is, just as I came to learn to avoid drunk white men outside pubs or the daggers contained in the eyes of old ladies yearning for the white Britain of yesteryear, I also learned to walk fast and avoid the eye contact of Muslim men. Often, this was made worse when the harassment was cloaked in the language of religion. Every Muslim woman I know has experienced a man coming up into her personal space, whispering 'masha Allah' as he undresses her covered body with his gaze. Or the 'salaam alaykum sister' shouted across the street accompanied by raised brows and leering smiles. In my teenage years, when I was just starting to learn about my faith, it felt confusing and frightening to see these men turn beliefs of mercy, equity and devotion into something twisted, something for their own carnal gain.

I think back to the early years of my hijab journey, and they are marred by the times I was made to feel small by the hefty gazes of men or feel like I hadn't sufficiently covered my body if they still found something to objectify.

Like the boys in McDonald's, desperately trying to capture my friends' and my attention as we sat pooling together the leftovers of our lunch money to buy a large fries and McFlurry between the three of us. As we chatted, giggled and deliberately ignored the eyes that we felt burning into our covered skin, the boys started to heckle us, clearly angry that we had rejected their advances. 'You're haram anyway, why you eating McDonald's? You call yourself Muslims? McDonald's is haram you know!' As though our religiosity was contingent upon us returning their interest. Obviously, the fact that they, too, were eating McDonald's had escaped them. But we were girls. This sort of thing was normal, wasn't it? Even if the rotten feeling afterwards burrowed itself in our bones, refusing to budge.

Or the security guard in Primark who was at least forty years old with a large, intimidating frame and eyes that looked down on me from above. I happened to once pass him whilst on the phone to my dad, speaking in Arabic. As soon as I hung up, he started pestering me, speaking to me in Arabic, too, even dropping things in my path as I entered the shop and then picking them up just as I approached to slow me down. Every time I entered the store (which felt like a lot in my teenage years in a dull town with nothing to do other than window shop), he would follow me as I browsed, asking me how I was, where I was from and what I studied (GCSEs, uncle). He spoke to me with a smirk that made my skin prickle and made me feel like curling up into a ball to escape it, as though even when ignoring him, just by existing, I was doing something wrong, giving him something that I didn't want to. I think back now and wonder why I didn't tell a member of staff, but then I realise that someone must have noticed this grown adult man following this teenage girl around the store and it can't have been only me he spent his days shadowing. Anyway, whenever I thought about putting it into words, I didn't know how. How could I articulate that mere small talk made me feel wrong and frightened all at once? So, in the end, I simply stopped going to Primark until he left.

Perhaps the most physically terrifying time was when I was on my way home from a late revision session at school. It was one of those afternoons in winter when the darkness hangs so low you can touch it, and it feels like the cusp of something dangerous. As I sat in the dank, urine-stained bus station in our town centre, waiting for the number 14 and silently going over my physics revision notes in my head, I tried to ignore the eyes on me that seemed to be scouring and searching, puncturing my outer layer to get inside. When the bus arrived, I got on with an old lady and a couple of men in high-vis vests and just before the door closed, on came the man who was watching me. On the virtually empty bus, he chose to sit right next to me. To this day I can recall the clammy warmth of his body close to my side, the mingling of sweat and cigarette smoke with the thudding of my frightened heart in my chest.

Once the bus set off, it began.

'Salaam alaykum sister...' He wanted to know my name, where I was from, what my hobbies were, complimenting my features whilst continuing to ogle me from barely a couple of centimetres away. He told me he was seventeen – although I knew he must be at least double that. He told me he was studying medicine at the local college, but last time I checked they didn't offer a BTEC in medicine at Northampton College. To seventeen-year-olds.

I tried to look out the window and was met with my own reflection, my crumpled school uniform in the fogged-up glass, and it made me feel sad, small and alone. I feigned interest in my phone: in the days before social media on the go, I clicked through texts I had sent my mum earlier about what we were having for dinner. I thought of texting her about what was happening, but then I remembered her warning to me, that Muslim men would harass me if I wore the hijab, and I didn't want to prove her right. So I kept quiet.

Once I took my phone out, that was like a red flag to a bull: he pushed and pushed for my number. I don't know how my fifteen-year-old self mustered up the courage to not give it, I think I just kept avoiding the question, but eventually he turned angry: 'I just want to check up on you. We are sister and brother. I'll say, "Salaam sister, how are you today?"' which then turned to 'Why won't you give me your number, bitch? I bet you give it to all the boys, so why not me? I bet you have a boyfriend, don't you, so why can't you speak to me?' His accusation that I had a boyfriend was meant to denote that he thought I was unworthy of honour, that I was immoral and promiscuous simply because I didn't acquiesce to his harassment.

The journey continued and as we neared my stop, the bus had all but emptied out. It occurred to me as strange that he was still on board, as mine was one of the last stops before the bus looped round again. I started to panic. I thought of the walk up the long and winding road to my house and how the streetlights had been turned off by the council, making it feel deserted and dangerous even at only 5 p.m. My parents were both still at work – only my younger brother would be home from school. I texted him 'quick – please come and meet me at the bus stop. I'll explain later. Come now.'

I pressed the bell for my stop and got up. He stayed sitting down and I had to squeeze myself past his knees to get out. As I walked towards the door, he quickly followed. He was getting off the bus with me. In the half-light of the street, I saw my brother there, and feeling my muscles slacken with relief, I rushed towards him. Only then did I see the man scuttle off in the opposite direction. In this random residential street, it was like he was exposed, his lowly intentions laid bare as he simply stood there – clearly lost where to go or what to do now. As an adult, I want to scoop up my tender teenage self and protect her from this situation. It petrifies me to think what would have transpired if my younger brother hadn't come to meet me – what would have happened to me on that dark street corner? And what does it say about the state of our entrenched violent misogyny, if all it took was the sight of a lanky teenage boy in a school blazer to send this grown man running in the opposite direction?

I am often frightened and appalled by the way misogyny and sexual harassment manifests within my community, especially given that the Qur'an mandates the opposite. Islam secures the right for women to keep their own names, wealth and property after marriage and explicitly outlaws forced marriages. As Muslims, our sacred text teaches men and women to interact respectfully and without objectification, lowering our gazes to avoid unwanted attention. And yet, on the ground, it feels as though some Muslim men believe that objectifying women is an irrefutable entitlement.

It seems to me that we are at the centre of a significant moment in British history – like we are witnessing the social rejection and self-destruction of feminism firsthand. Hundreds of women in Britain are killed every year – predominantly by the men closest to them. Social media saw a surge in vile misogyny spurred by the Amber Heard versus Johnny Depp defamation trial, with domestic abuse trivialised into memes and the suffering of abuse survivors commodified for likes and followers. At the same time, we are witnessing the trend of the 'tradwife', where women reject the supposedly feminist goals of education, employment and autonomy, aspiring instead to become housewives, purposefully inhabiting the very submissive, traditional role in the family structure that feminism is accused of turning its nose up at. These are usually articulated through videos (or even online courses costing hundreds of pounds) teaching other women how to catch successful, wealthy men for marriage, premised on the idea that making yourself obedient and docile is the way to secure these illustrious matches. Any female gender equality movement is vilified as a modernist scourge that makes women bitter, lonely and a traitor to our own biology. Muslims are not immune from this worrying current. I can think of multiple Muslim women with large social media followings who have started online courses teaching fellow Muslim women how to break free from the grasp of feminism and focus on making themselves good wives and mothers – totally sidestepping the irony of charging hundreds of pounds for such courses when their entire platform is built on a picture of Muslim femininity which thrives on domesticity, suggesting that the pursuit of careers and education, financial stability and independence go directly against the teachings of Islam.

The future looks more frightening still, and I worry about what this means for the next generation of Muslim boys and girls who are growing up under such a climate. Sometimes I look at my son, still in nappies, and wonder if I'll be strong enough to divert what seems like a tsunami of brutal misogyny ready to implant in his brain, absorbed through his fingertips from the smartphone he'll probably own at an obscenely young age.

Meanwhile, TikTok megastars like Andrew Tate, whose entire personas constitute a rabid hatred for women, are racking up billions of likes amongst young men and boys from all backgrounds – in fact, searches for these personas exceed the likes of Kim Kardashian and Donald Trump these days. But the issue seems particularly prevalent amongst Muslim boys who see this virulent strain of violent misogyny echoed in some of the warped interpretations of gender dynamics in the faith that surrounds them.

Videos from non-Muslim men with huge social media followings advocating for the rape and assault of women, comparing us to objects and denigrating us as shallow and materialistic, as naturally wired to serve men, and blaming women for their own mistreatment are seeing a worrying popularity amongst male Muslims of an impressionable age. Some of these non-Muslim TikTok stars even praise Islam and their Muslim followers, conflating the religion's clearly defined ideas around gender with their own oppressive and reductive patriarchal structures. And even though these men also advocate for things clearly forbidden in Islam like alcohol, gambling and adultery, their approval of Islam sends the message to young Muslim boys that Muslim masculinity is brutal and harsh and that women are objects to be controlled and consumed, afforded none of the rights that our faith guarantees us. It doesn't help when some mainstream Muslim platforms and even scholars with significant social media followings provide a platform for these characters to spout their sexist vitriol, thus inadvertently legitimising their views as somehow Islamic.

There's a corner of social media inhabited by Muslim men who view themselves as warriors against the ills of feminism, liberalism and modernism. Delve into this dark place and you will find clips of teenage boys saying their idols are both the Prophet Muhammad (peace be upon him) and the TikTok stars known for peddling such vile misogyny, even though the former upheld women's rights and the latter individuals are charged with horrific assaults against women. You will find men bragging about leaving their wives to go through labour alone because witnessing childbirth will make them sexually disinterested later on. You will see young boys and grown men attacking women on the internet for showing strands of hair or even their faces, accusing them of lacking in morality and their fathers of failing to adequately control their women. Men asserting that there is no such thing as rape within a marriage, men obsessed with polygamy and men advocating for so-called no-strings nikkahs – Islamic marriages in which men get all the carnal benefits of marriage whilst women forfeit all their God-given rights like financial stability. You will find laymen with no formal religious education twisting sacred text, removing the strand of gender equity that runs throughout our faith and instead warping the words to cement women's status as inferior and unworthy of respect.

There are other corners of the internet, too, of course. Ones where racism reigns supreme and Englishmen lament the apparent Muslimification of their homeland, posting incognito photographs of women in hijabs and niqabs for ridicule and pictures of the St George's flag reproduced in bacon, as though it'll make Muslims self-destruct at the mere sight of it like kryptonite. But in those corners of social media, I know what to expect. I can even laugh at the absurdity of it – screenshotting tweets about boycotting the bread in Tesco because it's halal and posting them on my group chats to laugh over.

But the dingy crevices of the internet where my entire humanity is refuted by men who share my faith, who are victims of some of the same Islamophobia I am, who might pray at my mosque or live on my street, feel more unsettling – and more disappointing. There is a particular, insidious betrayal that comes from seeing the men whom I should feel safe around bantering about rape and rendering Muslim women 'whores' for showing a portion of hair. A tangible fear runs through me to think that these are the men who Muslim women are forced to share community spaces with, to marry, to raise, to live amongst.

Being a Muslim woman feels like constantly agonising over what my oppression will look like today, which direction my denigration will come from this time. Will it be

Muslim men sending me rape threats for tweeting about a lack of prayer space at a certain mosque? Or will it be that far-right march through my town? Will it be white feminists wanting to liberate me from my hijab? Or the state stripping me of my citizenship, rendering me a second-class citizen? Either way, I'm stuck in that central reservation, and it doesn't matter which lane of traffic it will be that hits me, because from where I'm standing, they seem just as deadly as each other.

CHAPTER 4

SINISTER SAVIOURS

WHITE FEMINISM (AND OTHER LIES)

If, like me, you went to an all-girls' school, you know that's code for spending your formative years absorbing feminism whilst doing your eyeliner in the back of French class and sucking in your stomach in case anyone ever figures out it isn't concave.

In our Year 13 leavers' assembly, our head girl stood up on stage and said that our school identity ran through us all like a stick of rock, but really what we had all been imbued with was feminism. And why wouldn't we? All of the insanely high-achieving maths whizzes were girls. The Grade 8 piano maestros were girls. The Olympic-level javelin throwers were girls. The future gold medallists were girls. The honey-voiced choir singers were girls. The rich kids who owned ponies and mansions were girls. The sixth-formers getting scholarships for Oxford and Cambridge and Ivy League schools in America were all girls.

Success and womanhood are nowhere near mutual exclusives when your understanding of the world is what happens inside the gates of a girls' school.

Female councillors and businesswomen spoke to us in assemblies about breaking the glass ceiling and feminine strength. We studied literature through a feminist lens, learned love poems when other schools studied war. We had some random event where we all sang 'I Wish I Was a Punk Rocker (With Flowers in My Hair)' whilst we all... put flowers in our hair. Our local MP (Labour, a woman) came and told us every year or so we could do anything we wanted until the town voted in a male Tory instead.

I thought feminism was as indisputable as quadratic equations. I believed it like I believed my biology teacher when he taught us that our hearts have four chambers. More than that, I thought it was *for me* because, as we were told, feminism is for *everyone*. The future, after all, was female. History was *her*story now! I prepared myself for those glass ceilings that were going to need smashing, those male-dominated industries that needed infiltrating. I believed I could do anything and if anything stopped me, well, feminism was going to do something about it. Right?

In my mind, I think of the unravelling of my feminism as a major, dramatic, life-defining event, like getting a letter in the post that reads, *You know that feminism thing? It's not for you. Sorry!* But in reality, it was a gradual unspooling.

Whilst at school, feminism still ruled, but outside, the real world was starting to tell me otherwise. Slivers of truth revealed themselves to me when a department store manager asked me if I was 'planning on wearing that in front of the customers' when applying to work in their cafe as a teenager. When airport staff prodded my bun for explosives and casually asked me if I – a child – had ever been forced into marriage. When strangers with concerned, invasive eyes sat next to me on the bus and quietly let me know that I'd look much prettier if I let my hair loose.

Drip by drip though it might have been, the overall result was like being slapped in the face by a reality that looks entirely different to what you expected. To what you had been taught to expect. It struck me that what I had learned as *just* feminism in school was in fact white feminism: a type of feminism that concerns itself with nothing other than gender, that ignores the vital intersections of race, class and religion and how these conspire to compound a woman's experience of misogyny – especially in a state as hostile and divided as Britain. Feminism could do nothing for me when Islamophobia tainted people's view of me. When racist stereotypes told them I must be oppressed, coerced or a terrorist masquerading as a kid in Converses. White feminism, I soon learned, was great if some snotty-nosed boy comes along and says, 'Give me my ball back – girls can't play football!' It's perfect for getting a female President in office or banning Yorkie bars from saying 'not for girls'. But it starts whistling a tune and conveniently looks the other way when the misogyny *I* experience can't be cured with a smearing of pink paint, when it is defined by Islamophobia, compounded by being visibly Muslim, by being cut off from sources of power, privilege and whiteness.

White feminism has a major Muslim problem. In fact, visibly Muslim women pose a fundamental threat to the very standards that this feminism is founded upon. According to white feminism, liberation is found in the removal of clothes and the revelation of flesh. To cover one's body is fundamentally patriarchal, regardless of a woman's agency in the matter. Topless protests are the epitome of radicalism; burning your hijab in the street is the ultimate feminist move. It is the feminism of Pussy Riot, HeForShe and 'This Is What a Feminist Looks Like' T-shirts.

Covering yourself is what the patriarchy wants. It doesn't matter if the patriarchy also wants you to become a mother or to wear red lipstick and to smile. You can do those things and still be a feminist. But submitting to a God? A God who lays down rules, guidance and boundaries? That is, by default, sexist and oppressive no matter whether that person finds sanctuary in the act. No matter whether they chose it.

Women like me who choose to cover our bodies and hair, finding solace in not just the spiritual implications but the rejection of the male gaze, find our actions vilified by this dominant strain of feminism because all it does is replicate exactly what the patriarchy specialises in: removing our agency altogether.

This lack of autonomy paves the way for the kind of hollow representation politics that white feminism wrongly sees as the end goal. Hillary Clinton is a feminist queen. Suella Braverman and Priti Patel, Theresa May and Liz Truss are girlbosses if your only criterion is having the right chromosomes in the right places. Double points if there's a bit of melanin in there. White feminism cares very little about what policies these women might enact in office, or the views they espouse, because simply popping a woman into that seat is enough to quench its vapid presenteeism. If you don't see marginalised women as human enough to deserve dignity, you are blind to the fact that many of these aforementioned female politicians have made life actively more unbearable for women in the UK. Migrant and refugee women, single mothers, women in poverty and anyone visibly 'other' (like Muslim women) face the brunt of austerity cuts, hostile immigration policies and this cost-of-living crisis that keeps worsening. If your concern is a woman in the Home Office rather than the women giving birth in immigration detention centres or the ones drowning in the sea trying to get to Britain's shores, what is your feminism offering but upholding the status quo at best, and thinly veiled racism at worst?

That is precisely what makes white feminism so insidious:

it's an extension of white supremacy. Its Muslim problem is because it is so inextricably bound with racism and Islamophobia that prevailing stereotypes of Muslim women as oppressed and meek eclipse any recognition of us as self-aware, sentient beings able to make our own decisions. All gender equality goes out the window when it comes to acknowledging that a Muslim woman may choose to veil herself, because white feminism never gets beyond seeing Muslim women as repressed – and therefore in need of saving. Keeping Muslim women as victims crying out for a feminist to come along and unshackle them from their hijab is expedient for an ideology that is founded upon colonial ideals. White feminism is the age-old, racist, colonial ambition repackaged in pink. It is no different to what the history books tell us, to what our familial scars and our grandparents' migration routes tell us. It is the colonial dichotomy of superior secular, western values (read: white) liberating those poor and stupid Muslim women bound by patriarchy in faraway lands or under foreign deities. Like white supremacy, white feminism serves no other function than to dehumanise us and to feed the Islamophobia that is embedded into our world.

We see feminism's hypocritical liberal aims exposed at times when Muslims are being persecuted around the world. Feminist platforms which are so vocal about period poverty, domestic abuse or girls' education suddenly fall silent when Muslim women are being massacred at the hands of a western-ally state. Why? Because it doesn't fit white feminism's white supremacist end goals to see the dead bodies of brown Muslim women and children as a feminist issue.

Nowhere has the sheer visceral violence of white feminism been more exposed than in recent times as the death toll in Gaza skyrockets day by day. Motherhood platforms that decree that letting your baby 'cry it out' is a crime against humanity are deafeningly silent on the images of premature babies dying in bombed-out hospitals, their bodies decomposing as all fuel is cut off by Israel. Feminist figures whose hearts bled for Ukrainian women have nothing to say about Palestinian women having caesarean sections without anaesthetic. The piles of bodies in Palestine are not a feminist problem. Palestinian mothers wiping their children's blood off the floor because that's all they have left of them doesn't rouse the collective (white) feminist consciousness. Who is coming to save the Palestinian women going through pregnancy, menstrual cycles, labour, miscarriages, menopause with no water, with bombs flattening their homes over their heads? Not white feminism. No, we are never woman enough for their attention, perpetually othered even in our suffering, even in our destruction.

And even when white feminists do bother to glance

our way, they see us as perpetual victims, thereby disempowering and silencing us. This notion of Muslim women needing saving dictates the everyday lives of hijab-wearing women like me. It drowns out our narratives with a constant cacophony of *She's oppressed! Save her! Somebody save her!* Ask any visibly Muslim woman and she'll reel off countless examples of where this has played out. I could tell you about when I was a teenager on the bus and a very concerned-looking woman informed me that we were in Britain and therefore I didn't need to cover my head, or when my best friend's boyfriend added me on MSN to let me know he didn't think I should 'have to' cover my hair (thanks so much, Ryan, now that I have your approval, I can take it off!). When a teacher first saw me wearing a hijab and said, 'I didn't know your dad made you wear that' with a raised eyebrow. I could tell you of examples in my adult life, too – like a colleague asking me why I hadn't removed my 'head dress' now that 'Iran was free' (his words, not mine), or taking my son for a walk and hearing two old men lament about how 'you can barely tell you're in England any more' in our local area, loud enough for me to hear because either I don't speak English or I'm barely human enough to matter at all.

This prevailing notion of Muslim women in need of saving by white feminism not only strips us of our humanity but it positions us as recipients of feminism rather than active participants in it. It never asks us what we need or what we would like to benefit from. Rather, it tells us: to be enlightened is to uncover your head and reveal your bodies. If you do the opposite, you are oppressed whether you realise it or not. *Stepford Wives*, swanning around mindlessly in all that fabric and thinking it was a free choice to put it on. This is embodied in the 2023 Policy Exchange report entitled 'The Symbolic Power of the Veil', which speaks of Muslim women as children, ascribing us only enough humanity to acknowledge that we 'would say' wearing the hijab is an autonomous decision whilst offering the unspoken subtext that we don't have the capacity to even realise that we are under coercion in the first place.

White feminism has a white saviour complex at its core. It only registers Muslim women that fit into its definitions of victims. When Muslim women in Britain lambast racist barriers to participation or to accessing vital support, white feminism looks the other way. When Muslim women expound Islamophobic bias in the job market, hostile immigration policies, politicians calling us letter boxes or niqab bans, white feminism couldn't care less. But give it Muslim women whipping hijabs off and burning them in the street? Well, it starts licking its lips with delight.

Take Iran, in September 2022. Protests are erupting across the nation in response to the regime's brutal application of modesty laws – ignited by the murder of 22-year-old Mahsa Amini in police custody after she allegedly wore her hijab 'incorrectly' in public. Iranian women are bravely defying government restrictions on free speech to protest in the streets. Some are flouting the country's hijab mandate and removing theirs altogether, posting anonymised footage of themselves on social media with their hair uncovered in a country which bans such a thing. Other women keep their hijabs on and protest their sisters' rights to remove theirs if they wish – or to wear it differently to how the modesty police dictate. Religious necessity or not, they assert, the hijab shouldn't be a rod to beat women with by a state seeking to ensure absolute control.

The ears of the western world perk up. European leaders express their condemnation and governments call on Iran to be banned from the coming Winter Olympics. High-profile feminists post videos of themselves crying for the women of Iran. Instagram captions that might as well be entire think pieces pop up everywhere about hearts bleeding for the women forced to live under these modesty laws. Memes about men being afraid of the sight of an uncovered woman are commonplace. White celebrities shave their heads in solidarity and influencers livestream themselves dramatically ripping off and burning headscarves that they don't even usually wear anyway.

Anyone who cared about women's rights had something to say about Iran. Much of it was no doubt well intentioned.

Global struggles rely on international pressure to make a change. And as a Muslim woman who chose to wear the hijab, I would loathe having that choice taken away from me – for the state to dictate what I wear and how. My own family history of living under Gaddafi in Libya is etched vividly enough in my mind to know that any state that uses violence against its own people is authoritarian and barbarous. But much of the global reaction felt muddied and flat, void of critical thinking or nuance. It was white feminism, white saviourism, at play, conflating the right to choose how and whether to cover up with protests against the hijab itself as a garment and a symbol.

As usual, the Muslim women of Iran were never asked what, precisely, they were protesting for. It didn't matter to white feminism because that image of women stripping off their scarves, burning them in the streets, shaking their heads and loosening dark, lustrous curls was far too tempting to the orientalist imagining of the Muslim woman finally being released from her cage. At first glance, it was every Islamophobe's dream: this great unveiling of the Muslim woman. Evidence that they, the superior secular west, were right all along – given the choice, Muslim women would remove the shackles of the hijab. See, we told you, to be uncovered *is* inherently more progressive than being covered.

In the aftermath of the Iranian protests, I could barely open a social media app without encountering crude memes shared by people who had never before expressed any particular concern for the welfare of Muslim women. Random French actresses and that girl I sat next to in Year 9 food tech posting pictures of 'before' and 'after' Iran, showing miniskirt wearing, heavily eyelined, bouffant-haired women (smiling, happy, free) next to a faceless mass of fabric (sad, oppressed, *Muslim*). The truth is that an authoritarian regime happened between those two images. But the subtext to the person who doesn't bother to engage with the politics or the context is that this is Islam. Look what it does to women.

I say that white feminists have no time for the subtleties and complexities on the matter, but the truth is that white feminism leaves no room to even fully conceptualise the Iranian case and has little appetite in bothering to anyway. It is too rudimentary, too black and white a system to understand the nuances. Iran doesn't fit into its good guys versus bad guys pro forma because this comes down to choice. Women wanting to wear the hijab but demanding it be their own *choice*. Wanting to remove the hijab and that being an acceptable, legal *choice*. But the word 'choice' is missing from the white feminist dictionary when it comes to Muslim women, because it's something it conveniently forgets we even have.

Because white feminism refuses to think of Muslim women as autonomous, the case of Iranian women is now being inaccurately applied the world over – to the further detriment and dehumanisation of Muslim women in places like Britain. The aforementioned Policy Exchange report, 'The Symbolic Power of the Veil', features a whole chapter on Iran – indeed the whole report is inspired by the Iranian hijab question. It mentions 'Iran' 286 times and 'Muslim women' only eighty-nine. The report, and the white feminist ideologies that it is guided by, dangerously extrapolates a very specific set of political and social conditions in Iran onto Muslim women worldwide – including in the west. The call of Iranian women to end state brutality, to halt the regime's use of violence against its own people and its erosion of women's bodily rights becomes warped into a far-right argument to view the hijab itself as the problem. The state enforcing it or the means by which it is mandated in Iran become irrelevant.

Time and time again, the report speaks in these white feminist, reductive dualities of good versus bad, free versus oppressed. It talks of 'oppressive dress codes' without ever asking who gets to say what is oppressive and to whom. It throws around vague statements straight out of the white feminist playbook, like 'the absence of the veil is invariably a mark of resistance'. Without even a hint of critical commentary, the report's predominantly white male authors give legitimate arguments offered by Muslim women themselves and then whitemansplain why they're a load of rubbish. Take this, for example:

A common defence of the veil in the form both of the hijab and the niqab against western criticism is that it is a matter of personal choice for a woman, in the same way as any other item of clothing. If western (or indeed non-western) women can choose to wear Oscar de la Renta, Armani, Dior, Gucci, Stella McCartney, Zara or Whistles, why can't a Muslim woman choose to wear a headscarf or even a full body covering? This is, of course, to confuse categories, misrepresent Islam, its protocols and codes and discount the way in which Islamists deliberately situate the veil within an oppositional 'paradigm of authenticity'.

Got it – if you defend your right to wear whatever you want, you're an Islamist. Unless you're defending your right to wear Armani – then you're fine.

It's no coincidence that the report sees codes that force women to cover as oppressive but not ones that force them to uncover. That's white feminism in action. For all the white feminists who shaved their heads, cried on camera and burned random bits of cloth they'd never worn, there was nothing but tumbleweed silence when exactly a year after the Iranian anti-hijab protests, another state enacted a law equally as restrictive on the bodily rights of women.

France. The land of liberté, égalité, fraternité. Home of the revolution and the city of love. Croissants and berets, chic little cafes and Islamophobia. In September 2023,

France took its already incredibly committed long-term relationship with dominating Muslim women's bodies to a new level by banning abayas in state schools. Other highlights in this decades-long love affair include banning hijabs in public buildings in 2004, prohibiting niqabs in 2010 and its ever-expanding vendetta against not wearing a nice little bikini at the beach – also known as burkini bans.

Though ostensibly an abaya ban, this latest piece of legislation is really a further criminalisation of Muslimness itself. At the time of writing, schoolgirls across France are being turned away at the gate for wearing not just abayas but anything vaguely resembling one – including high-street maxi dresses and Japanese-style kimonos worn over jeans and a T-shirt. Videos leaked by students and their families have shown that the very same teachers blocking the girls' entrance to school are sometimes wearing similarly long-sleeved, ankle-length dresses, too – probably because garments like these hang up in pretty much every high-street store in the western world now. But on middle-aged white women, an H&M maxi dress is innocuous – trendy even. Loose and comfy, perfect for the hot weather. But on a child racialised as Muslim – with the wrong kind of name or slightly too-brown skin – that same dress is perverse, archaic and, above all, now illegal.

Girls being turned away at the school gate because of how they are dressed sounds dystopian. Like some *Handmaid's Tale*-esque vision of overt, nonsensical patriarchy

– although, of course, the author of that particular piece of oft-referenced literature preserves *her* judgement for places that mandate head coverings, not ones that ban them.

Can you imagine a British school telling girls that to get through the school gates they need to show more flesh, to cover less of their bodies? Hike up that skirt a little bit and you can run along to English class, Emily. It sounds absurd – creepy, even. If a teacher said that, they'd probably – hopefully – find themselves sacked and on some sort of register for life. Rightly so: when schools in Britain have imposed racist restrictions on certain hairstyles, they have faced criticism from local communities and even student protests. School dress rules are supposed to create a veneer of equity, not erase the identity of one group altogether until, by force, they succumb to being the same as the rest.

Girls' access to education is high up there on feminism's list of concerns. When a nation like Afghanistan restricts girls' access to school, naturally, the world is in uproar, because all children should be allowed an education. You can't really consider yourself a feminist unless you think girls should be allowed to go to school. And yet, when the French state embeds into law that in order to obtain an education, female students must show *more* of their body, there is silence. There is no mass feminist reaction. There are no international gender equality organisations calling on France to allow all girls an education. No European governments are proposing to invade or bomb France into allowing Muslim girls through the school gates.

My timeline is free of random celebrities wearing their best Zara maxi dress in solidarity with the Muslim girls of France. Some minor B-list actor is not crying on TikTok about how France can control the bodies of children this way. I'm not sure about you, but I haven't seen anyone burn a miniskirt in protest of France's mandate that you must show your legs to get an education. The reaction is depressing, infuriating, but it is predictable. Muslims defying the state to cover up doesn't fit white feminism's mould of what is progress and what is oppression.

Dig into the specifics of this French anti-abaya law and the preposterous hypocrisy at the heart of white feminism is laid bare. Like all of France's policing of Muslims, supposedly this is about equality – or égalité. State buildings are secular, and a hijab is a religious symbol. But it is no coincidence that French feminists were some of the most vocal proponents of the 2004 hijab ban, famously banning covered Muslim women from their meetings, and some of the loudest advocates for the state-enforced notion of secularism. Others affected by this ban – including nuns – are not routinely dehumanised. They do not navigate a paradoxical position of being both victim and threat. Though masquerading as secularism, this legislation – like all limits on Muslim women's bodies – is about taking white feminism's preoccupation with saving us and entrenching it into law.

The anti-abaya law falls apart as soon as you look close enough at it to see it for the Islamophobia that it really is. What, fundamentally, is the difference between an abaya and a maxi dress, other than who is wearing it? Hijabs are already banned at school, so French teachers and leaders can't even use the presence of a head covering to presume that the dress is functioning as an abaya rather than a fashionable high-street garment. The only factor between one girl being let through the school gates and not another is how these students – these children – are being racialised as Muslim. Criminalised by virtue of their name, their appearance or their perceived Muslimness.

Muslim women's bodies are the battleground in which the war against Islam is fought in Europe. France's long history of suppressing and culling Muslimness stems from its colonial past. It did the same in North Africa, sending postcards of veiled women with exposed breasts home to French men to advertise the Maghreb as a cornucopia of mysterious, tempting covered women – encouraging them to come along to the Orient and rape its women, slowly turning it French, turning it white.

This abaya ban is simply part of its continued colonial agenda and ironically, at the same time, a reaction to a problem of its own making. You don't invade and pillage your way to being the second largest empire in the world without the progeny of the people whose homes you destroyed coming to you – the so-called motherland – for a sense of stability for generations to come.

If white feminism cared about Muslim women beyond the possibility of unveiling us, the French problem would have white feminists rapt and angry. Muslims in France are already incredibly materially disadvantaged. Islamophobic legislation, police brutality and structural racism culminate to force Muslims into poverty, into living in ghettos or *banlieues* and out of work. A 2022 study found that if you are a Muslim woman wearing the hijab in France, you have a 1 per cent chance of getting a job. If you are identified as Arab or African, you will spend twice as long on social housing waiting lists as anyone else. The European Islamophobia Report of 2022 named France as the world's most Islamophobic country. In this context, to create a specific barrier stopping Muslim girls from accessing school should be a feminist issue of global proportions.

If white feminism viewed the resistance *to* wear the hijab the same as it views the resistance to *not* wear it, it would see that stopping girls getting an education is to use women's bodies as a political battleground. It is to destroy the future prospects of young girls now so that poverty is perpetuated through the next generation later, thus keeping Muslim communities disenfranchised and disempowered for years to come.

Justifiably, when a state uses women's bodies to score

points, win votes or assert power, white feminism comes up in arms. When the US Supreme Court overturned *Roe v. Wade*, the entire world mourned this loss of women's bodily autonomy, and this wave of grief was led by white feminists at the helm. Major believers in the white feminist cause made lazy, stereotypical comparisons to countries like Afghanistan. *This is not the Middle East! This is America!* A meme showing the Supreme Court judges dressed like the Taliban (or just generic Muslim men, take your pick) did the rounds on social media. The message, of course, being that you can do what you want with Muslim women's bodies but not *ours*. Not our white bodies.

In the same way that white supremacy relies on fabricated biological essentialism and the assumption that some races are inherently, scientifically, inferior to others, white feminism, too, doubles down on the shaky notion that some women are just more likely to succumb to patriarchy than others – because they know no better.

In our patriarchal world, are any of us free of its pervasive grasp? Do any of us truly and completely operate outside of its reach? Why, then, are Muslim women's decisions seen as being influenced by patriarchy – sometimes without our own awareness – whereas all white, all western, all non-Muslim women are acting of their own free volition?

Last time I checked, none of us get to say 'Sorry, but I'm choosing to bypass the glass ceiling directly. Straight to CEO for me!' Saying, 'Sorry, sir, but I've actually opted out of patriarchy, so you don't get to objectify me in the street! Too bad!' is no more an option than withdrawing your consent for racism. It affects us all differently, but patriarchy is universal. It is embedded in the systems that govern our lives: our laws, our institutions and our public bodies. And whilst some women experience a patriarchy that is admittedly far less compounded by race, class or religion, it is never the case that any woman gets to just navigate her life without patriarchy ever subtly dictating it for her.

Take clothing – whether it's high heels, miniskirts, make-up or push-up bras, the way women dress is almost always rooted in patriarchy, whether we acknowledge it or not. Whether it's a manmade algorithm subtly influencing our buying habits, marketing execs in grey suits sitting in a boardroom and deciding which garment is fashionable this season – whether through the fashion industry, the media or straight up dictated by the state – can we ever really say how we dress isn't somewhere along the line derived from patriarchy?

Why, then, is a woman choosing to wear a miniskirt assumed to be autonomous whereas one choosing to wear an abaya is, by definition, brainwashed? Wearing high heels to work even though our feet ache, showing cleavage, applying make-up or waxing our legs – even though it's time consuming, uncomfortable and sometimes even painful – all of these are considered innocuous, autonomous choices made by free humans, even though in truth their origins lie in patriarchal beauty standards applied to women. When we were teenagers, none of my friends were stopped by passers-by to let them know they didn't *need* to wear those hot pants that were impractically and uncomfortably short. Nobody informed them they were free to cover up because *this is England, and we are all free, don't you know?* I've never been asked whether my husband dictated I wear winged eyeliner or blusher and I'd hazard a guess that very few women have been stopped on the Tube to be asked whether some chauvinistic male boss is making them wear those high heels. And yet, all of the above – and more – is put to visibly Muslim women every day, as we go about our daily lives.

If white feminism isn't concerned with saving women from the high heels or the miniskirt but *is* set on saving us from the hijab or the burka, the only conclusion to this double standard is racism. And this means it becomes less about which women are free of patriarchy and which aren't (none of us are) and more about which *kind* of patriarchy is better. Which is less oppressive, less violent? Less overt, more acceptable? Which kind of patriarchy is worthy of global headlines and military occupations? Which is harmless, the prerogative of a sovereign state?

That's the thing: just as white feminism patronises Muslim women, it also vilifies Muslim men. In their eyes, not only are we innately prone to brainwashing but our husbands, fathers, brothers and sons are uniquely controlling in a way that other men are not. White feminism relies upon this dichotomy: if Muslim women are the ones in *need* of saving, it's Muslim men and their uniquely backwards strain of misogyny that they need saving *from*. White men in suits enacting laws to curb women's bodily freedoms might be ultraconservative, yes, but bearded brown men doing the same thing are barbaric, draconian, primitive. White governments enforcing clothing laws onto children that prevent them accessing school are simply acting in the name of equality and secularism, whereas Muslim regimes banning girls from going to school are archaic. Governments mandate their female citizens must cover their heads and global outrage ensues. Governments dictate that female citizens must *un*cover and nobody bats an eyelid. In fact, it's all good in the name of secularism. White feminism needs Muslim women to remain perpetual victims just as much as it needs Muslim men to be especially and uniquely patriarchal – and for this misogyny to be an imported, foreign force. A force that needs eradicating. And there, at that very point, white feminism gives way to white supremacy and lets it do its thing.

White supremacy is a global export: it has to be for it to function as a political tool. It compels women around the globe to bleach, straighten and shave their way to European beauty standards; it creates hierarchies of colourism in non-white communities; it makes white migrants expats and brown ones parasites. It champions one universal, emanating truth: that proximity to whiteness is power. And its best weapon, white feminism, has been traded and transported across the world, too, like a commodity sold for profit.

Even in Muslim-majority countries with sizable secularist movements, and especially those seeking political contiguity to the west, white feminists are watching Muslim women. Take Turkey, where hijab-wearing women can find themselves abused or even assaulted in public for covering their heads despite mosques being on every street corner and the adhan sounding five times a day. In fact, under its secularist agenda, hijabs were banned entirely from educational institutions and in public buildings until 2013. In some sections of Turkish society, covered Muslim women are seen as a symbol of regression to an archaic past, of selling out to Arab states and as the absolute antithesis of the enlightened European. Sound familiar? You don't need to be white to embody white feminist ideals.

Given both Turkey's repeated attempts to enter the EU and its geographical proximity to major warzones like Syria (and, as a result, a high concentration of refugees and migrants from these areas), the public perception of the veiled Muslim woman has become inextricably linked with these political tensions – just like how in the British context, the hijabi comes to symbolise the Islamification of Europe and the erosion of a British identity. For a group stripped of so much agency, visibly Muslim women face a disproportionate amount of political attention and interrogation – and that's because by virtue of covering our heads, we flout all of white feminism's laws. Much of the hysteria from other European nations around the prospect of Turkey joining the EU has centred on this image of the covered Muslim woman infiltrating European lands. Perversely and contradictingly, she is both threatening and oppressed – unable to stand up to some chauvinistic husband or father but at the same time intent on turning beautiful blonde-haired European women into faceless entities swathed in black cloth. This paradox is of white feminism's making and finds its way forming the foundation of policy and social attitudes across the globe.

Likewise, Turkey's own secularist and anti-refugee movement, which surged during the recent 2023 general election, is preoccupied with the image of the veiled Muslim woman, featuring hijabis and niqabis on its large campaign posters across the country next to slogans about kicking out migrants and keeping Turkey for the Turkish. Wherever we are, the veiled Muslim woman is seen as a political token – a harbinger of some latent threat or a warning of what is to come – but never truly her autonomous self. Though largely made up of women who would consider themselves progressives and liberals, white feminism begins to sound more and more like the extreme far right – and that's because for Muslim women, it might as well be.

White supremacy is not simply about superiority. It is a crusade of contempt, of utter disgust, of domination. White feminism pitying us would be one thing, but it also hates us – loathes us in a way that you can only loathe something lower than you, like a nasty little cockroach beneath your shoe. Some of the biggest names in the British white feminist wall of fame barely manage (or bother) to conceal their hatred towards Muslims in general and particularly Muslim women. Journalist and author Melanie Phillips, who continues to be regularly platformed on our television screens despite her anti-Muslim views, wrote a book called *Londonistan* in 2006 in which she called Islamophobia 'the thought-crime that seeks to suppress legitimate criticism of Islam' and to this day continues to call Islamophobia 'bogus' and nothing but 'fiction'. Phillips has penned reactionary and inaccurate articles claiming Muslim women attempt to defy the iron fist of British justice by hiding behind face veils, peddling that myth that beneath the layers of fabric, we are victims, perverse tricksters and terrorists in waiting all at once.

Writer and columnist Julie Burchill, another of white feminism's favourite faces, had to pay substantial damages to journalist Ash Sarkar a few years ago when she publicly accused her of 'worshipping a paedophile' and being an Islamist (Islamophobic trope? Tick) as well as ridiculing her for supposedly having a moustache and being a victim of female genital mutilation (racist misogyny? Ding ding). Burchill even wrote a poem fantasising about sleeping with Sarkar and far-right French politician Marine Le Pen, as if you needed any further evidence that if you pity something long enough you grow to hate it. This dynamic, between Sarkar, who is not visibly Muslim other than having brown skin, and Burchill, a white woman, replicates the very same position that all women of all races are subjected to by patriarchy at large. To be mocked for your physical appearance, undermined by virtue of your biology and bombarded by crude and violent sexualised remarks is exactly what women face at the hands of men. Except us Muslim women have to pre-empt and fear this coming from white feminists, too – and just imagine how much more perverse and dangerous those attacks are for women who, unlike Sarkar, *are* visibly Muslim, who cover their heads and bodies. Muslim women are the price that white feminists have paid for their power – we are the thing they have traded for their status. The suffrage of today's feminist ilk is not changing laws or breaking barriers – it is the right to reproduce the same patriarchal structures we have always been dominated by, but this time to be on the side of perpetrator rather than victim.

Julie Bindel, another self-professed 'radical feminist writer', possesses what can only be described as a career-long obsession with what Muslim women wear. Writing about the hijab and niqab for decades, she has referred to it as 'the tyranny of the veil' and 'Islam's totalitarian tendencies'. In true white feminist style, she has called upon her fellow feminists to stop being so 'shamefully silent' on the issue of Muslim head coverings – and, yep, you got it, she blames Muslim men for stifling the debate and labelling anyone an Islamophobe as soon as they dare speak up. Bindel's ideology perfectly encapsulates the paradox of white feminism's double fixation on Muslim men as savage thugs and Muslim women as docile subjects. In 2018, she wrote about how progressives like her 'capitulate' to 'hardline Muslim men' if they refuse to speak up against the veil. Not only does this push Muslim women out of the picture altogether, to create a battlefield between enlightened white feminists and angry chauvinists with beards and skullcaps in which both sides are fighting over Muslim women without ever asking us our own thoughts, but this deliberately and conveniently obscures what the political situation in the UK is like for British Muslims. Muslim communities are disenfranchised on every level – politically and materially, socially and financially. In housing, in employment, in healthcare, in education. Today, half of all British Muslims live in poverty compared to around 18 per cent of the general population. To claim that 'hardline' Muslim men somehow possess the power or the capital to dictate the free speech of women like Bindel is nothing but a racist fallacy. Muslims are rarely seen on our television screens unless we're winning a gold medal, a baking contest or playing some reductive caricature of ourselves for cheap laughs, whereas white feminists can be found proselytising almost weekly on *Woman's Hour*. If white feminists see the label of Islamophobia as a barrier standing between them and calling out the veil, why is it automatically the work of fictionalised despotic Muslim men sticking a tape over any woman's mouth who dares utter the word 'hijab'? Maybe it's us visibly Muslim women ourselves saying, *hey, white feminists, we are not in need of saving.*

CHAPTER 5

LETTER BOXES

HOW ISLAMOPHOBIA IN BRITAIN IS GENDERED

In 2015, when a teenage girl ran away to Syria with a head filled with lies and dreams and two friends by her side, she likely never realised that her name would become a racial slur, that her face would become synonymous with the latent threat that Islam supposedly poses to the west. She probably never foresaw that for years to come, her veiled, faceless form would occupy the front pages of tabloid papers, that her name would drip off the tongues and fill the minds of grown men fixated on retaining the Britain of yesteryear. How could she, a mere teenager, have known that she would cease to be herself any more at all? That she'd morph into a symbol of something so much bigger than a kid from Bethnal Green: a harbinger of British social collapse, the bogeyman of the far right. A great massive *I told you so* to proponents of multiculturalism everywhere.

If you want to see how Britain treats its Muslim women, look no further than the case of Shamima Begum – even when, at the time, that Muslim woman wasn't a woman at all but a child. And even when that child was a British child, who was groomed by a grown man. A man who, as it happens, was a double agent selling insider terrorist intelligence to western states. Even then: she is other, she is foreign, she is a veiled threat.

In this book, I've written a lot about how my experience of misogyny is defined by my visible Muslimness. But not only is misogyny compounded by racism and Islamophobia; the opposite is true too: Islamophobia in Britain is highly gendered. Islamophobia affects Muslim men and Muslim women differently, in manifold nuanced ways. But there are certain specific barriers that Islamophobia saves especially for Muslim women, forcing us to navigate not just Islamophobia in every facet of our everyday lives but *gendered* Islamophobia. And that makes it all the more pervasive, all the more consuming and all the more exhausting to be on the receiving end of.

Islamophobia is gendered for Muslim men too, albeit in different ways. Muslim men face the repercussions of long-held colonial prejudices casting brown men as primitive and inherently violent: sexual predators threatening to spread their brown, Muslim seed around these enlightened white lands. Take the recent Home Secretary, Suella Braverman, and her factually incorrect claim that 'almost all' perpetrators of child sexual exploitation are 'British-Pakistani' men who bring views that are culturally 'incompatible with British values' into the UK. Despite evidence showing time and time again that sex offenders in the UK are most commonly white, high-profile cases like Rochdale fuel arguments that all Muslim men are child groomers and rapists. This version of Muslim masculinity which pervades the far right (and increasingly the mainstream, thanks to a government happy to peddle it, too) dehumanises and brutalises Muslim men until they become worthy victims of physical attacks on the street and racist border policies that see them withering away in immigration detention centres for years or being deported halfway across the world to be somebody else's problem. Where Muslim men are concerned, Islamophobia's great campaign is to conceptualise every Muslim man as dangerous, like a cancer to be eradicated from the body of the nation.

For Muslim women, the ways in which our Islamophobia is gendered is perhaps more nuanced – more complex and, frankly, contradictory than it is for Muslim men. If Muslim men are savages, we are their victims. So we are repressed and submissive. But, at the same time, we are considered treacherous and malevolent, too – at least when it is convenient. Fully grown Muslim women, it seems, can't really choose to wear a hijab of their own free will (we must be coerced, even if we think it is our choice), but a Muslim child *can* make the fully conscious decision to run away to join a terrorist organisation – even if the whole thing was arranged by a man on the internet. When it suits the system and the state, we are damsels in distress dying to be saved, and the rest of the time (especially, it seems, when we could actually do with a little humanity), we are terrorist masterminds suddenly autonomous enough to be in charge of our own minds and bodies.

From every conceivable angle, every single development that has unravelled since the Bethnal Green girls first fled to Syria in 2015 has encapsulated one thing: the hysteria and the utter hostility that the British state – and much of the public at large – holds towards Muslim women. From that initial, pixelated footage of those three children walking through airport security, to Shamima in a refugee camp begging the NHS to save her dying baby, to being told with a journalist's camera shoved in her face that she has been stripped of British citizenship – the only place she has ever called home. It's impossible to view the entire case with even a semblance of impartiality and not see the double standards and hypocrisies glaring back at you like cat's eyes on a night-time country lane.

I was nineteen, a few years older than Shamima, when she and her friends followed a man's instructions and got on a plane and then a bus and eventually crossed the border into Syria. Mass hysteria gripped the nation. But what I saw on the inside didn't match what I was witnessing on the outside. At home, my dad watched the news incessantly, intermittently turning to me with grief-stricken eyes as if to check I was still there. 'What her parents must be going through,' he'd mumble, shaking his head. Amongst my Muslim friends and family, there was overwhelming concern, anxiety, trepidation – like all communities experience if ever a child goes missing, but especially if that child has gone to meet a grown man somewhere unknown. At the time, I was halfway through my English degree and volunteering at a local primary school in preparation for eventually training as a teacher. In the staff room, someone mentioned a student with a Muslim name and how she hadn't come into school that day and another teacher made a joke about how we'd better make sure she hasn't run off to Syria, too. Everyone sniggered and avoided my eye. Years later, as a qualified teacher, I'd sit in safeguarding training as a massive picture of Shamima's veiled face was projected across the school hall. 'Keep this image in your heads,' the morose Scottish woman would say: 'this is what happens if you don't report something that doesn't seem right.'

The news was dominated with voices already projecting her fate – calling for her to be imprisoned if she ever returns, demanding she be turned away at the shore, debating her agency in joining a terrorist organisation as a child. 'How could you not know your child is a terrorist?' I remember one anchor saying down the camera, as though anyone really knows what fills the inside of their teenager's head. The press referred to them as 'jihadi brides', both adultifying and sensationalising them at once. Not victims of grooming or teenagers in the midst of an albeit catastrophic mistake – but jihadis. Terrorists. Criminals.

Where it seemed that the public had defaulted to assign blame, I remember feeling an intense sadness at the whole thing – something I know was replicated in the uneasy stomachs of my female Muslim friends, too. Now that her first name alone is synonymous with 'terrorist', it's not a particularly fashionable thing to say, but I have to be honest and say that I saw myself in Shamima. I thought of myself at fifteen – in fact, even then at nineteen – and I knew I could have been lured in by shiny ideas of acceptance, love and excitement, too. What kid doesn't want that? When I was Shamima's age, I was slap bang in the middle of an identity crisis to rival anyone in middle age. I felt like I had no true friends whom I could be myself around. No place to fit in, nowhere I quite belonged in my entirety. I was still half-clinging to the idea that I was British – white, even – and yet the eyes on me (and what was on my head) wherever I went told me I wasn't welcome any more, even if Britain was all I had ever known. If someone had come along in the middle of all that and offered me a utopia where everyone looked like me, where people would love me, where I could live independently and have those adult things little girls dream of like a family of my own and money to buy the things I want, I probably would have been tempted, too. Yes, because I was lonely, confused and tired of the weight of Islamophobia already but also because I was a teenage girl and to the eyes of a fifteen-year-old, someone caring about you enough to pay for you to travel halfway across the world can look a lot like a fairytale.

I can't speak for Shamima, but what I can say is this: whether it was the social media age of today or the size-zero-is-king fashion magazines of my own adolescence, there is already a specific, indefinable sense of isolation that comes from being a teenage girl. Of growing into a body that you don't understand the power of yet and that others think they have a birthright stake in. Of moulding yourself to fit into beauty standards before you've even finished growing into the person you're meant to be. Hormones, misogyny and societal expectations all collide in those tumultuous first years of womanhood and it is exhausting. Add to that the experience of being visibly Muslim in Britain – of having the wrong shade of skin or a covered head and body when everyone around you is first experimenting with showing theirs. Being othered and finding that nobody has taught you what to do once you're left on the other side.

Traversing ground that your parents never have before because they came as migrants. Growing up with your entire cultural references being derived from a country that is increasingly sending you the message that it isn't home after all. Code-switching entire dialects, whole versions of yourself between school and home to try to fit in.

Assuming you were British because you were born here but seeing your foreignness reflected back at you in the eyes of people on the street. Parents telling you that *it doesn't matter, this isn't our home anyway* and wondering how home can be anywhere other than the only place you've ever known.

It was another world entirely growing up before diversity and inclusion became a *thing*, before hijabi influencers hit the mainstream, before it was possible to look around and see someone like you doing something other than scrounging for benefits on the front of a tabloid newspaper or some terrorist's wife. When misogyny was in its size-zero-is-the-only-acceptable-size and sexual-harassment-is-something-to-laugh-about-on-national-TV era. When social media wasn't yet ruling our very existence, but you always had to be ready in case your friend tagged you in a photo on Facebook. When racism wasn't quite so frowned upon as now and people made jokes about bombs in your bag or Bin Laden being your dad. When maxi dresses weren't in high-street shops and wearing anything longer than hotpants was treated about the same as stepping outside in a bin bag. When I think back to myself as a teenage girl amidst all that, I'm tempted to say I'd accept a way out if I was offered it, too.

Perhaps that's why some of the only people I've seen even willing to entertain the notion that a young woman who was groomed as a child shouldn't be made stateless by the only country she has ever known are fellow Muslim women – because we know what comes before, what lies beyond the extremities of isolation, disenfranchisement and otherisation. Maybe because the only ones bothering to see the humanity of Muslim women are us Muslim women ourselves.

Unpack everything that has happened since Shamima Begum first stepped foot on a plane to Turkey in 2015 and you'll see that it is inextricably rooted in Islamophobia. Of course it is. At the time, the police chose the opportunity for surveillance on Muslim communities over its duty to safeguard British children when it failed to respond to the growing issue of radicalisation and simply handed out leaflets to school kids instead (anyone who has ever known a child will attest to the fact that leaflets just end up crumpled at the bottom of a school bag). It's difficult to see the police exercising such a response if it was white British children suddenly running off to join a cult abroad, but the default of the British state when it comes to Muslims is always to criminalise – even when that puts us at further risk. Even when children are involved.

Similarly, the *should she be allowed to return?* debate that has racked the nation for years and erupted almost as soon as the girls stepped through passport control reveals how the British public really sees us. If whether a Brit should be allowed to return home is even a question worth asking, that spells out one thing: our Britishness is always conditional. White 'native' Brits can commit crimes and never see their Britishness called into question, but for British Muslims and ethnic minorities, our place in this nation is always dependent on whether or not we play nice. How well we integrate. Whether we acquiesce. There's no room for teenage mistakes or falling victim to grooming as a child when you have to constantly prove that you're worthy to stay in the country you were born in.

Above all this, though, if you're looking for evidence that Britain's treatment of Shamima Begum is undeniable Islamophobia, look no further than the fact her British citizenship was stripped in 2019 after all. Or that almost 80 per cent of the British public agreed with that decision. When then Home Secretary Sajid Javid (ironically of Muslim descent himself, although famed for saying, 'The only religion practised in my house is Christianity') rendered Shamima stateless, he set a precedent. There are two types of Britons: those whose family trace back to the Anglo-Saxons with surnames like Smith, Green and Jones, and those whose parents, grandparents or even the generations before them came from somewhere else. If you're the former, the great news is that you're stuck here regardless of whatever you might find yourself embroiled in. If you're the latter, you can be made stateless because even if you've never been there before, there's some other country somewhere that can technically have you if Britain kicks you out. And just like that, a two-tier system is created between the *real* Brits and those allowed to stay here as guests as long as we never do anything wrong. This precedent has since crystallised into a law so dystopian and racist that it should alarm us all: the Nationality and Borders Act 2022.

Shamima was a British child when she was groomed in her British bedroom. She went to a British school. She was born here – indeed, she has never been to Bangladesh, but by virtue of her parents being from there, the state was able to make her somebody else's problem whilst conveniently skirting any of the blame for why a British child could have found herself running off to a warzone in the first place. British-born ethnic minorities like me are now faced with this perverse threat – dominated by the knowledge that the place we thought of as home isn't really home at all if it can evict us at any given time.

But Shamima is not just the victim of an Islamophobic state that refuses to see her as a once-groomed child – or even as a British problem to be brought to justice. She is the victim of an Islamophobic state that is governed by systemic misogyny as well. Her vilification in the eyes of the nation, the media and the press is not simply because she is Muslim but because she is a Muslim *woman*.

Visibly Muslim women cannot escape this fate. We are bound by our gender identity as much as we are drowned out by what is on our heads. In a patriarchal system built for and by men, all women have to quickly learn how to stay afloat. We make ourselves palatable and quiet, polite and not too domineering. We hide demands in niceties and second-guess ourselves, adding 'no worries if not!' to the ends of emails when we would absolutely worry if not. We make ourselves pretty because that means we are heard and seen in a society that barely registers anyone who exists outside the definitions of conventional beauty. We suck up the PMS pain and the menopause symptoms and go to work anyway, so as not to be an inconvenience. When faced with a police force infiltrated by rapists, we form our own solutions to being unsafe at night, texting friends our locations and staying on the phone until we're home. But Muslim women have to double guess whether that creepy man is going to call us a terrorist or sexually assault us. We infuriate a system that demands access to our bodies by covering them up. When the male gaze is used to getting what it wants, it doesn't know what to do with women who refuse to cater to it entirely.

If Shamima Begum was a man, or if she was considered more conventionally attractive in the eyes of whichever artist is doing the cartoons for certain racist tabloid papers, she wouldn't be caricatured in the gormless, animalistic way she so often is – portrayed with very obviously racialised features like exaggerated lips and massive, soulless eyes. Until recently, whether by donning swathes of black cloth, being make-up free or wearing the clear impact of unthinkable trauma on her face, she had committed the ultimate crime against patriarchy: to not appeal to the male gaze. And Britain – whether the general public, its leaders or the state – cannot comprehend sympathising with a woman who flouts its patriarchal notions of beauty.

When Muslim women are considered palatable enough to appear on our screens, it is only when they fulfil at least some of the criteria of what this deeply racist, inherently misogynistic nation wants to see in women. No one is inviting niqabi women on primetime TV to talk about the effects of certain policies on Muslim women. Women who dress in ways perceived to be less overtly Muslim are platformed to speak about issues that affect veiled women the most. Women who do wear the hijab are acceptable if they pair it with so-called western clothing and make-up, turbans and shorter sleeves. That's all fine – but never bare faces and abayas. Whether it's Boris Johnson calling niqabi women letter boxes, David Cameron saying our 'traditional submissiveness' is why our children are falling into terrorism, Iran's anti-hijab protests or France's abaya bans, the events that define us are constantly debated on our screens without visibly Muslim women's voices ever being heard. Women who tick the boxes of having brown skin or Muslim names but have never experienced how it feels to be otherised because of their clothing, who know nothing of the visceral threat of gendered Islamophobia, are passed the mic instead and our voices are drowned out.

But ironically and tragically, Shamima Begum's attempts to play into these patriarchal codes have failed, too. In line with her efforts to sanitise her image in the public's mind, we have watched her through news interviews and documentaries gradually unveil herself. Niqab to red hijab to tank top. Black cloth to blonde highlights and baseball cap. Ever cynical as this nation is when it comes to Muslims, though, even this has been met with widespread suspicion and derision – despite this being what Britain demands of all its Muslim women, really. To unislamify ourselves and prove our integration through our bodies. The press accused Shamima of using her uncovered shoulders as a publicity stunt, her new western makeover as a way to keep herself relevant. This, we were told, was evidence of her perniciousness. Like some sort of insipid shapeshifter, she was trying to pull the wool over our eyes by sneaking back into England with all the other young women in vest tops and shorts. Telegraph columnist Allison Pearson wrote an article entitled 'How stupid does Shamima Begum think the British public are?' in which she describes her transformation from 'the defiant, black-clad young woman who described the bombing of the Manchester Arena and the murder there of twenty-two innocents as "justified" into a polished and contrite media performer in western clothes, albeit one with highly convenient amnesia'. Let's think about that: *in western clothes*. Playing a role that she has no right to inhabit. Always, always *other*. According to not only the right-wing figures that rule our media but almost 80 per cent of the British public, she's had her chance to be British. Now it's too late.

I don't – I can't – share this scepticism. Seeing Shamima gradually British-ify her appearance simply makes me sad, like watching a jester do a silly dance for cheap laughs whilst their face belies their misery. It reminds me of what all of us Muslim women inherently know. No matter what we do, it is never enough. We cannot ever fully be victims because we always pose a latent threat. We cannot ever fully be British because our dress, our skin, our DNA will forever be foreign. This paradox that dominates our world traps us in it, keeping us forever suspended between being too many contradictory things at once – someone's political symbol and someone else's mascot.

Any woman recognises that pressure to prove your humanity through your body – to absolve yourself of that specific strain of blame that is only ever reserved for us. Would a Muslim man accused of terrorism ever be objectified this way? He would certainly be pressured into ridding himself of his Muslimness, ditching the thobe and getting a fade haircut to look a little more palatable to the court of public opinion, but would he be hypersexualised? Simultaneously pressured into and then judged for revealing skin? It barely warrants clarifying that the response is a resounding 'no'.

Shamima, like all of us Muslim women, cannot escape the fact that she is both a woman and Muslim. And it strikes me that it is precisely *because* she is a woman that her punishment is to languish statelessly, aimlessly in some refugee camp in a forgotten place. If she were a Muslim man, the nation would thirst for blood – or images of her behind bars. Great British justice prevailing and holding her to account. But she is a woman, and so her retribution is gendered, too. For Shamima, Britain chose that her sentence was for her babies to die, unable to access the help of the NHS because of their mother's actions. Her suffering is to perpetually beg on television for the state to reconsider, to have her grief televised for all to see if she wants to remain relevant at all. Britain has Shamima Begum where it wants Muslim women. Begging for mercy. In a constant state of subservience to the state's superiority. Powerless. Making herself ever less visibly Muslim and that never, ever being enough.

Women in general are expected to be ceaselessly grateful. But for women of colour, and especially Muslim women, this is heightened to new levels. A Muslim woman who is not positively tripping over herself in gratitude is not a Muslim woman that the British state or public has any time for. Whenever winner of *The Great British Bake Off* Nadiya Hussain has tweeted about being the victim of Islamophobia, her replies are flooded with people telling her she should be grateful to be here at all – that she should go back to Bangladesh if she doesn't find England to her liking. When Nazanin Zaghari-Ratcliffe was finally free to return to the UK, she was accused by some of not being 'grateful' enough to Britain for 'freeing' her, despite it taking five Foreign Secretaries to do so and Boris Johnson's false claims about why she was in Iran in the first place adding years to her detention. The blame was even laid at *her* feet by one ex-Tory MEP who questioned why she went to a country with 'such a nasty regime' at all. *Send her back* trended on Twitter. Even being British, even being a victim, is never enough when you're a Muslim woman constantly charged with proving your own right to be here, your own humanity.

Like all misogyny, gendered Islamophobia manifests through fetishisation, too. There's a reason why, for the past decade, one of the most highly ranked performers on Pornhub has been a hijabi. Or, rather, a Lebanese Christian former adult actor who rose to fame for starring in pornographic videos wearing a hijab. The racist, violent sexualisation of Muslim women sells in an inherently patriarchal society that cannot handle the notion of a body it can't see or control. From the colonial fixation on unveiling the Orient to hypersexualised AI-produced images of Muslim women today, and from Victorian artwork portraying harems full of voluptuous figures beneath swathes of cloth to war photographers taking photographs of beautiful Muslim women in the midst of conflict, as though we are only worthy of sympathy if we happen to have piercing green eyes, the fetishisation of Muslim women is pervasive, far-reaching and it sells.

Make no mistake though, fetishising us does not ascribe us humanity – in fact, it simply deepens our subjugation. The popularity of so-called hijabi porn in the west (it racks up the highest viewing figures in the USA) is precisely because hypersexualisation is another form of domination. Like a political colonial conquest reimagined as rape. Muslim women in public positions face this crude sexualisation and obsession with unveiling us to see what's underneath not from people who *like* Muslim women but from people who hate us. This fetishisation is rooted in hatred rather than appeal. You only have to look at how rape is used as a weapon of war to see that it's about control and abhorrence.

Nadiya Hussain of *Bake Off* fame is routinely told by trolls on the internet to remove her scarf to show everyone what's underneath. Recently, a Muslim fitness blogger who has started to wear the hijab has seen her comments flooded with men thirsting over the notion of getting under the layers of her clothing, bragging that they still have screenshots of what she looked like before. Shamima Begum is as regularly the butt of racist jokes as she is of hypersexualised ones. The highly gendered, hypersexualised punishment that the west covertly threatens Muslim women with is to get under the physical barriers that we construct around ourselves. It's almost as though the notion of a veiled Muslim woman is simply so infuriating to the western imagination that the only way to get around the fact our bodies are hidden is to hypersexualise us instead – as though to say, *you can hide yourself, but there's nothing you can do to stop us imagining what's underneath.*

It's not even as though you could argue that visibly Muslim women play any active part in the phenomenon of hijabi pornography to begin with – not as though that would make the entire thing less dehumanising. From the leaders of the industry to the actors partaking in the content, from the ones who make money, careers and platforms out of the fetishisation of the veil to those who gratify themselves off of our objectification, visibly Muslim women are missing from this entire equation. Our image is abused, our identities co-opted for someone else's gain and the result is simply to bury us in further stereotype, deeper violence and greater silence. And yet, even though we have no agency in the entire charade, we do bear the brunt of its repercussions. Regardless of how much or little power individual adult film stars may have in the industry, the fact remains that they get to take the hijab off at the end of the shoot and go about life without any of the criminalisation or brutality, with none of the pity or suspicion that follows those of us who are visibly Muslim in public every day. For women who look like me, on the other hand, even though we played no part in it, the violent hypersexualisation of hijabis is now immortalised on the internet to such an extent that it shapes how people see us, how we are treated and the uniquely sexualised, gendered Islamophobia that we are subjected to.

Muslim women don't get to choose when to be hypervisible or not. We don't ever get to blend in unless we succumb to Britain's ideals of femininity and remove our hijabs altogether (and even then, see Shamima Begum to know that that will never be enough). But those synonymous with hijabi porn get to elevate their own careers whilst treading on the bodies of Muslim women to get there. These days, Mia Khalifa, who has recently moved away from the adult industry, is the latest boss babe of white feminism. In 2023 she appeared on the front of *Huck* magazine under the headline 'We are all Mia Khalifa' (*are we?* I wanted to say) and was even invited to speak at the Oxford Union. She, and the industry that made her, have paid no price for what it has done to Muslim women, and Khalifa's repeated refusal to apologise to hijabi women is testament to how we are only ever an object: a ladder to propel someone else's career, a veil to be worn and taken off when it suits.

Speaking of objects, let's talk letter boxes, shall we?

Letter box, *noun*
1. A box attached to an outside wall, or a slot in the door of a building, into which mail is delivered
2. A veiled Muslim woman, according to the former British Prime Minister

See also: bank robbers

Given the fact that he communicates almost exclusively in a near constant babble, it's likely that Boris Johnson's now infamous 'letter box' analogy was just another throwaway comment in a career full of them. He was trying to convey how ridiculous, in his eyes, it is for a woman to choose to go about with her face covered, like a letter box, a ninja or whatever other slur is aimed our way on an almost daily basis: *towel head, rag head*... You get the gist.

But here's the thing: I'm an English teacher which means I'm condemned to a life of reading 'the sky is blue' and being convinced it illustrates melancholy, so I can't help but see a letter box as a symbol of something more. In one fell slur, Johnson showed us exactly how the nation sees Muslim women. And even if he meant it specifically about women who wear the niqab, all visibly Muslim women have felt its force. In the week following his *Daily Telegraph* column, incidents of Islamophobia rose by 375 per cent. Tell Mama, the leading organisation in the UK for monitoring anti-Muslim hate crimes, reported that in the three weeks after the article was published, 42 per cent of the offline Islamophobic incidents it saw 'directly referenced Boris Johnson and/or the language used in his column'. Muslim women with even the most minor of public platforms were bombarded with memes likening us to letter boxes. Even now, if I open my Twitter DMs after I've written an article that's particularly critical of the state, there will often be a letter box in there somewhere.

Letter boxes are passive, silent, mute things. They linger on streets and corners, and you barely notice they're even there at all – invisible to eyes trained to look past them. They are uniform and homogenous – you can't tell one from another because *they all look the same.* Of course, they don't really. Some are more square and some are round, some adorned with little quirks like spikes on top. But you never bother to take in the nuances when you're walking on by. You just take for granted that they're all one indistinguishable mass. Letter boxes stand open and submissive, ready to receive post, rubbish or cigarette butts from whoever wants to stick something inside, expected to take it all without ever objecting. They're purposeful, functional entities – great for getting that document across the country in a couple of days but not much else. Not really anything to look at. In fact, rather menacing in the dwindling light of evening: a dodgy figure, stoic in the distance. They are plonked down in a place and stay there for decades, for generations without ever stirring unless with someone else's permission, to serve someone else's aims. But letter boxes are also pervasive – there are hundreds of thousands of them across the UK. Go out looking for letter boxes and you'll be able to see nothing but. You'll be convinced they are taking over, leaving no room on the street for anything else. Letter boxes are unequivocally – iconically – red. Red. The colour of sensuality and sin. The colour of blood, danger and death. All these things at once, all the time.

All that calling Muslim women letter boxes has done is create a mascot for the same gendered Islamophobia that has prevailed for eternity, or since white men first saw veiled women. It exposes the rotten, hypocritical heart at the core of Britishness itself, that sees an entire demographic of human beings as so lowly that we aren't really human at all. Muslim men are shackled by Islamophobia, rendered nothing but angry bearded thugs, but at least they are seen as people in their own right – albeit chauvinistic, primitive ones. But Muslim women? We are the thing your dog stops to pee up the side of. The thing you walk straight on by. Barely one step up from a rubbish bin. Apparently.

CHAPTER 6

INVISIBLE

MOTHERING WHILST MUSLIM

The air is damp and thick and smells like washing that's taken too long to dry. The smacking rain outside has fogged up the bus windows, which means I can't quite tell which specific road in east London I'm trudging down, but I'm willing to ride it out because my son is finally, finally asleep. Slowly, slowly I retrieve my phone from under the hood of the buggy, careful not to wake him. I turn off the white noise app – the rain is doing the job for me. I've got 5 per cent battery left to distract myself from my postpartum mind that swings from death to delight to dinner in a matter of seconds.

I text my friend, 'Found the cure to racism: have a baby lol' and she replies with an emoji that indicates she isn't about to wave goodbye to racism any time soon.

When I first sat down next to the woman beside me, I was sure she was about to either tell me to go back to where

I came from or propel herself so far away from my overt Muslimness that she would become one with the side of the bus. You learn to pre-empt it, you see. That lingering glare. The gaze taking in the hijab, the abaya, the foreignness of it all. Of you. The pursed lips and puffed out chest, ready to pounce in case I whip out my Taliban loyalty card or self-combust at any given moment – like them Muslims do.

But rather than racist abuse, or a loaded sigh, it was 'ahh isn't he gorgeous!' that I was greeted with instead. And I smiled in biased agreement as her steely face melted, giving way to the unmistakable nostalgia of a fellow mother. We chatted, then. About motherhood and babies, the joy and the pain of it all. We spoke in the way, I've learned, mothers do when we recognise a fellow soldier in the trenches – someone you don't have to say 'oh, it's the best thing I've ever done' through gritted, unbrushed teeth, ignoring that weird feeling that makes you permanently five seconds away from crying.

As the bus chugged blindly through the rain, she told me her kids ignore her now and how I must cherish these fleeting, special months, and I promised to absolutely do so whilst I prodded my tongue into the tenth ulcer my son's skull had graced me with that week. She advised me how I should have another child quickly so they can play with each other and how I must make sure I ask for help when I need it and I nodded, entranced by this perfectly average woman's captivating wisdom. And then it was her stop. She gathered her shopping bags and buried a racist newspaper under her arm and squeezed herself between me and the buggy, whispering 'mustn't wake the little fellow!' as she went. 'Ooh, what's his name by the way?' she asked, whilst the bus halted in traffic and I told her, and when she didn't seem to register, I told her again, louder this time. And over two remarkably uncomplicated syllables, her face dropped and the stern look returned, 'Oh, pity, couldn't you have picked a nice English name?' and off she went into the rain.

I texted my friend, 'Never mind. Even that doesn't work.'

Strangely, new motherhood and wearing the hijab have a lot in common. Yes, the former involves a whole lot of nappy changing and getting beaten up daily by the small human that you carried for nine months, whereas the latter could involve anything from being called a terrorist on the Tube to being routinely mistaken for that other hijabi who worked in the same building five years ago. But at their core, both motherhood and the hijab render women invisible to a society trained to overlook us, unable to recognise that we still exist under a headscarf or behind a pram.

For all the waves of feminism that we have traversed and despite how liberal and progressive the west claims to be, Britain is still a highly pronatalist society. In fact, this is the case in many western nations where policy and legislation are created to place the mere possibility of a baby above the bodily rights of the woman. Women who inadvertently provoke their own miscarriages have been prosecuted. Women's right to abortions, even in cases of rape or medical emergency, are being curtailed. Female politicians without children are still seen as cold and unfit for high office. Women childless by choice are viewed as selfish. We wrongly consider it to be the preserve of the monolithic 'east' to be preoccupied with childbearing, perpetuating the position of women as nothing but baby machines, but even the most so-called enlightened societies remain in the business of procreation: our world will never tire of the need for the next generation of workers.

Before girls are anywhere near puberty, they're nudged towards motherhood. The toy industry teaches girls child-rearing when they're still children themselves. Whereas boys' clothes bear slogans of adventure, discovery and bravery, girls' clothes tell them to be kind and smiley. Peace, love and chill vibes all round – in other words, be acquiescent, meek and nurturing like good little mothers-in-training. We are introduced to the ticking of our biological clocks as soon as we get our first period. Ominous algorithms spawn social media adverts telling us to freeze our eggs by our mid-twenties, as casual as plugging a pair of trainers.

Yet, despite the system's every effort to push women into motherhood, it offers no cushioning once women do find themselves on the other side of that cliff. And it's no accident that I call it a cliff. Motherhood is by far the most all-consuming, life-changing, defining and unravelling act a woman can do. To have another life grow inside of you, to nearly break your own body to bring that human into the world and to then forever experience the gradual and enormous grief of them being separate to you is like giving birth to your own heart and watching it exist as its own entity. To go between wanting to cocoon them inside your own skin for safekeeping to desperately craving the freedom of being your own person once more. It is as exhilarating as it is terrifying, lonely as it is validating. In every sense of the word, it is a cliff into the unknown. And it is by design that the system disappears from view at the exact moment women need it to step in and support the very motherhood that we are trained to inhabit from childhood.

What the system truly values is our reproductive potential – not the inconvenience of feelings and leaking breasts, maternity rights and affordable childcare. The situation for mothers in Britain at the moment is dire, and that's because motherhood erases the woman entirely to the point that she fails to be considered a person at all. Society has a need for wombs, not for the women who own them, and you can't build policy around a group of people you don't even register to begin with.

It starts as soon as you declare your pregnancy to your GP. You go along for your first scan and in exchange for a coloured folder which will contain all of your maternity notes (mine was orange) you lose your name. You become 'Mum'. Even if you are not yet anybody's mother – certainly not the mother of the fifty-year-old midwife who is calling you 'Mum' even though your name is right there on the screen. In every appointment from then on, you'll be spoken to paradoxically as if you are both a child and already an established mother. *Are you eating properly, Mum? Come and pop yourself down here, Mum. OK, I'm going to examine you now, Mum. Mum. Mum. Mum.*

This loss of identity prevails in every facet of your life. Your career will be stalled if not halted altogether and poor (or non-existent) maternity pay will probably mean you are living on a fraction of what you used to earn despite now having an extra mouth to feed. After maternity leave, you'll be faced with the impossible choice of either placing your baby in a nursery that will guzzle practically your entire salary just so you can return to work, or giving up your career altogether and being considered unemployed by a society that only values paid labour – despite the fact that you got to sit down a lot more in your day job than you ever do looking after a toddler all day at home. Oh, and whichever one you choose, people will judge you for it.

Adverts and the health system will bombard you with slogans like 'breast is best' without ever explaining how to manage near constant breastfeeding whilst earning money to keep a roof over your head or having some semblance of your own identity. Social media influencers will shame you for feeding your kid a fruit pouch or sticking them in front of Cocomelon whilst you cook dinner or (heaven forbid) have a ten-minute break. Employers will skirt round the legal restraints to figure out whether you're about to pop out another baby a year into a new job, and you'll come back from maternity leave to find that a man called Steve, who started a month ago, has already been promoted over you. In public, strangers will ask you if you have considered feeding your inconsolable child (as if the thought had never crossed your mind), they'll push past you to get on the bus first and God help you if you get on a plane and your child dares to cry because you might well find yourself going viral, accompanied by comments about how mothers today are just too lenient with their kids.

Of course, there are dazzling, unrivalled beauties in motherhood, too. Of loving something so much you could puke, cry or laugh. The rare joy of picking up leaves in the park or watching an aeroplane go by. A chubby palm on your cheek and perfectly mispronounced words, belly chuckles and sleepy cuddles. But the common denominator in the things that make motherhood hard is a society that fundamentally fails to see that there is a woman behind all that mothering. There is a career that meant something before she had to give it up because nursery is too unaffordable. A woman whose mental health is affected by inadequate postpartum care, the eradication of Sure

Start centres or poor maternity pay. A person doing all the domestic drudgery that keeps households, families and communities functioning.

Through coming to terms with my own invisibility as a mother, I realised that I was already invisible anyway. Not because the hijab itself suppresses me but because our hypersexualised society erases me, as a hijabi. It has no language for, no interest in humanising women like me who defy society's standards of womanhood. No amount of feminism eradicates the fact that women, the world over, are judged by their bodies, preceded by their appearance, in competition with beauty standards we can never attain.

Getting to the highest office in the land doesn't stop magazines running close-up shots of our crow's feet or bat wings. Even the most crucial political questions of our time don't distract from the prevailing societal obsession with women's bodies – like that now infamous *Daily Mail* double-page spread comparing Nicola Sturgeon and Theresa May's legs, reimagining the Brexit debate as the 'Legs-it' race.

When everything is built around and catered to the male gaze, those that exist outside of those boundaries simply don't register at all. In my experience, you realise you are now invisible pretty much as soon as you start to wear the hijab. People don't bother to look at your face. They see the cloth and immediately call you the name of some other hijabi they once knew – even if you look nothing alike. In public, people bypass you – serving others before you even though you were waiting long before them. People push in front of you, your questions fall on deaf ears, people don't even meet your eye as though you're a not-quite-human thing. It's like people don't know how to comprehend a woman whose body they can't see, whose hair they can't examine, whose figure they can't make out – a woman they don't have automatic access to with their eyes.

Now, as both a mother and a visibly Muslim woman, this double invisibility follows me wherever I go, like navigating the world as nothing but a floating hijab pushing a buggy – altogether void of the woman behind both façades.

Long before I ever considered becoming a mother, I knew where I was going to spend my maternity leave. It's telling, it occurs to me now, that I thought of maternity leave this way. Like some sort of Victorian noblewoman planning which country house to spend the summer season in or which seaside town to while away my melancholy. I suppose I hadn't imagined the domesticity of it – do we ever truly dream of labour?

It was the middle of lockdown where the only thing to do was to fight over toilet roll in the middle of Tesco or suddenly take up exercise so you could leave the house. My husband and I had taken to driving to a postcode far more expensive than ours that had a large green overlooked by a neat square of Victorian houses with pastel front doors and black and white tiled paths. A semi-dilapidated gothic church stood close by like a dormant relic. If you ever get the Central Line almost all the way to the east, you'll catch a glimpse of these houses from behind as they reveal the jagged extensions stuck on the back like spaceships ready to take off. From the front, you'd never imagine what's on the other side.

We'd get takeaway coffees and walk around the green, peering past the 'thank you NHS!' rainbow signs into front rooms that hung fine art above the mantelpiece instead of TVs. We'd amble through the churchyard and feel the old stone crumble as we touched its walls. We'd wander down the high street, past the closed shops, wrinkling our eyes at passers-by so they got the message that we were smiling behind our facemasks.

On one of these afternoons, when things were starting to open up, my husband paid too much to get his hair cut in a faux Victorian barber's shop by a man with an ironic moustache and tortoiseshell glasses because I'd done such a bad job of cutting it myself. I sat outside on the slanted bus stop seat and watched what I can only describe as a procession of perpetually pregnant yummy mummies in dungarees and Vejas pushing thousand-pound buggies. Everywhere I looked, there were children, babies or very skinny women with enormous pregnant bellies. Infants sprouted off bodies like unruly limbs, bobbing up and down on the shoulders of Birkenstock-wearing dads or zipped inside their mothers' puffer coats.

I was starting to become preoccupied with the idea of becoming a mother myself, suddenly playing catch-up with my resurfacing childhood notions of what being twenty-six should look like. Mesmerised, I watched Scandi-dressed toddlers with perfect mops of blonde curls run after immaculately styled mothers sipping impossibly small coffees. I watched them swing an assortment of organic vegetables in a net bag from their wrist and stop to chat to people in the street, throwing around phrases like 'little Tarquin', 'piano tutor' and 'seven plus'.

I felt like I was being given a glimpse of what the next phase of my life should – and would – look like, and I envied them like a child envies an adult who gets to stay up late and eat as much chocolate as they want. And from then on, I dreamed about babies and motherhood almost every night. I followed women on Instagram who went for brunch with their newborns strapped in £300 Artipoppe carriers on their front. I could have told you all about baby-led weaning, the fourth trimester and gentle parenting long before I had any use for those things myself.

Lockdown persisted, and we continued to come to this specific green with that specific high street, and I silently plotted out my early motherhood days. In my head, motherhood was the series of frothy flat whites in hip cafes that I saw every time I now opened Instagram – it entailed little more than cuddling a docile baby who does nothing but chuckle cherubically and being always impeccably dressed in an incongruous combination of fitness gear and something oversized. I saw myself pushing a ludicrously expensive pram, stopping to browse the organic squashes or spend a fiver on a loaf of sourdough like it was nothing. Like that Victorian aristocrat relocating to the country for the summer months, this was the stage on which I was going to enact this illustrious role of mother that I felt was slowly coming into reach.

Like most high streets of this kind, this one is encrusted with harbingers of gentrification like an ironically named butcher that sells artisan meats, an independent grocery store and a Gail's Bakery wedged between a JoJo Maman Bébé and an M&S Food. Perfect, right? I didn't let the fact that I had never frequented these places before stop me from having it all planned out. I was going to sip hot coffee and watch the deciduous trees slowly burn orange across the street, making friends with other mothers without even trying because I'd be part of whatever special club giving birth grants you entry into. I'd get through a novel in a matter of days – maybe even write one – whilst my son slept soundly, strapped to my chest. Or so I told myself.

When I did eventually become a mother, I quickly realised that it's not all browsing the free-range eggs whilst your obedient child recites Latin verbs aloud for all to admire. In fact, it's not that at all – at least not for me. What I had come to see as universal motherhood was actually only a specific, privileged, unattainable type: the preserve of the middle class, the rich and, mostly, the white. After all, if you've got a night nanny, you might just find yourself with enough wherewithal to browse the craft cheeses on the street corner or enough vivacity to put together an outfit that wouldn't be amiss at London Fashion Week. If you don't have to worry about racism for not just you but your child too, you might be a bit happier, a bit more free to not pre-empt whether someone's going to hear your baby crying and hurl racist abuse at you. The type of motherhood I had idolised isn't universal at all – it is simply the systems that rule our world perpetuating themselves in the next generation, playing out full circle. Navigating new motherhood under the myth that the baby in my arms was enough to grant me entry into this exclusive world was just that: a myth. Because whiteness, privilege, power and wealth don't go on maternity leave.

When I did the things I imagined myself doing as a new mother, they had lost the sheen my mind's eye had attributed to them because I didn't fit in this world I had told myself I could slot into. In M&S Food, the security guard follows me around the store and asks to search the bottom of my buggy in case I've nabbed a pot of organic hummus. Every time I go into the Gail's I had envisaged myself in, a white man talking too loud on the phone about stocks and shares pushes in front of me in the queue and nobody even notices. My son would wave and smile at other babies whose mothers just looked the other way, and a woman came and handed me her empty tray and was almost about to ask me to clean the table before she realised it's unlikely I'd be halfway through a shift with a baby strapped to my torso.

I wonder now why I ever thought I'd be able to sit at what is essentially the adult version of *that* table in the high school canteen – you know, the one that housed all the mean, pretty and rich white girls. Hadn't I got the message that whiteness and privilege is built to exclude women like me? But where else are we shown aspirational motherhood? What other image of motherhood are we shown that is positive and that doesn't look shiny, stable and secure (and rich and white)? Our society vilifies mothers who dared to get pregnant without the cushions of wealth and privilege to support them whilst never bothering to question the man who played a part in bringing about that baby, too. Women who rely on benefits, who have multiple children and no job and no partner are presented as the lowest of the low in our media and by our politicians. This version of motherhood haunts the front pages of tabloid papers and inspires exploitative, voyeuristic television shows like *Benefits Britain* and *Benefits Street*. It lays the foundation for government policy that caps child benefits to stop women gaming the system, as though anybody is putting their bodies through nine months of pregnancy, days of excruciating labour and eighteen years of caregiving for ninety quid a month. Even television programmes that are supposed to poke light at the gruelling demands of motherhood normalise wealth, whiteness and privilege to such an extent that you'd be forgiven for believing those were prerequisites for procreation. Take BBC's *Motherland*, where the women's biggest concerns are their builders charging them too much for redecorating their gigantic houses or husbands who spend too much time at their six-figure-salaried job.

Perhaps I idolised this unattainable vision of motherhood because I had rarely seen Muslim motherhood up close – certainly not a British iteration of it. Being neither brown nor Muslim, my own mother didn't have to navigate visible Muslimness whilst stumbling through the tumult of early motherhood. My aunties in Libya who I'd spent my childhood summers with operated in a different world entirely. One where children walked from one open door to another and where everyone just sort of vaguely mothered whichever children were in front of them, content that the others would be cared for by a neighbour or sister treating them as their own. I hadn't really seen first-hand what it looks like to balance the physical and mental demands of motherhood with visible Muslimness, with structural racism, with the double jeopardy of misogyny and Islamophobia following you wherever you go.

In the things we read and watch, Muslim motherhood

is rarely given a platform – and if it is, it's almost never with any real nuance. When we do see Muslim mothers on our screens, they constitute nothing more than the archaic backdrop to a protagonist's search for freedom – the oppressive, strict home from which they yearn to be free. We are shown women surgically attached to the kitchen, whose dreams extend about as far as their daughters marrying doctors, or silent and subservient victims of patriarchal codes that are depicted at odds with western ideals. We are shown women who hover in the background. Women who suffer at the hands of misogyny or themselves perpetuate it. Women who spend all day gossiping about so-and-so's child who did this or that. Women who are flat, one-dimensional archetypes – symbols of outdated and damaging ideas.

Whilst comedies like *Motherland*, though imperfect, at least manage to portray mothers as exhausted yet accomplished and imperfect yet empowered whilst still retaining humour, there is no equivalent for Muslim mothers. In Britain, the icons and representatives we Muslim mothers are given are Zainab Masood of *EastEnders*: so out of touch and parochial that she doesn't realise her daughter is whipping her hijab off every night and getting pregnant in club toilets or that her son is having an affair with a man. We get *Citizen Khan*, whose portrayal of a Muslim mother is someone who is perpetually cleaning and in a constant competition with what her friends' husbands are buying for them. An infantilised financial burden on the patriarch, Mrs Khan is relegated to nothing but endless nagging with no concerns other than going on holiday to Dubai and her daughters having lavish weddings. There is Javed's mum in the 2019 film *Blinded by the Light,* who is little more than a symbol of the regressive traditionalism from which her children long to escape in search of liberation. The 2020 film *After Love,* which won Joanna Scanlan a BAFTA for best actress, obscures the humanity of the protagonist Mary Hussain altogether. The thwarted, frumpy victim of bigamy, her matronly hijab-covered form is juxtaposed against the sensual, liberal Europeanness of her husband's lover who mistakes her for the cleaning lady when they first meet. Muslim mothers, Muslim wives, Muslim women are never ascribed a voice of our own. We are simply the foil to reveal someone else's actions: the cruelty of our husbands, the freedom our children crave, the archaicness of our cultures. Our own subjugation.

Since becoming a mother, I have searched in longing for something to validate the indefinable frenzy that motherhood is. Something that spells out the ugly truths and heady joys of motherhood through the lens of Muslim women. Where are the women on my screen navigating breastfeeding or potty training whilst dealing with institutional Islamophobia? The comedies about returning to work from maternity leave into industries which are rife with structural racism? The dramas about overcoming postpartum depression featuring women that look like me? They don't exist because *they* – be it society at large or whoever's in charge – don't see us to begin with.

As ever with Muslim women, we are never *just* invisible. If we were, perhaps things would be a little easier. After all, a system that doesn't see us can't police us, can't surveil us, can't suspect us with one hand and try to save us with the other. But no, as always, our invisibility is contrasted with the simultaneous threat we pose. Our wombs are the vessels for the next generation of Muslims. We carry within our very biology a ticking time bomb that the far right are convinced is about to detonate. A Britain, a Europe, a west that looks different. That looks, sounds, behaves, eats and speaks *Muslim*. We hold the threat of this in our bodies, in our ovaries.

If, like Enoch Powell or whichever racist has a keyboard today, you fear for a Britain in which hijabis and halal butchers are on every high street, really you fear Muslim mothers and what we might hold in our wombs. So as invisible as we are to the public and as disenfranchised as we are by the state, we are also hypervisible to an anti-terror machine with a vested interest in what we do with those bodies we're hiding away.

In 2016, Prime Minister David Cameron pledged £20 million to help Muslim women learn English. Specifically *Muslim* women. Not Sikh, not Hindu, not Jewish women. Muslim women. As though language inaptitude is somehow linked to religious belief. According to Cameron, 38,000 Muslim women at the time did not speak English and over 190,000 had limited skills in the language. For context, that is roughly 0.3 per cent of Britain's population in 2016. So why funnel so much money into a scheme for less than 1 per cent of the population? It's theoretically nonsensical to promise money to solve a problem partially of your own political creation – austerity cuts to community services and Sure Start centres had seen programmes like free English lessons for migrants slashed in the first place, after all.

But the answer revealed itself in the rest of the speech. Us feeble-minded Muslim women weren't to blame. Our inaptitude wasn't our fault – it was because, as the Prime Minister so tactfully put it, 'some of these people have come from quite patriarchal societies and perhaps the menfolk haven't wanted them to speak English'. As if that wasn't quite bad enough, Cameron went on to say that whilst he had no evidence to suggest so, he felt that non-English speakers might be 'more susceptible' to extremism. If we can't speak the language then we might not integrate properly and so might wake up one day and decide to join a terrorist organisation, or something like that. And yet, at the same time, it was this 'traditional submissiveness' of Muslim women that meant young Muslim men are falling into radicalisation. After all, mothers who don't speak English might not understand that their son is about to run off to join ISIS, presuming instead that he was just off on a Duke of Edinburgh trip to Syria.

Now, the gargantuan mental jump that is required to get from point A to point B in that ideological gulf aside, let us unpack this a little. What Cameron said in this speech lays bare the hypocritical paradox that dominates narratives of Muslim women – and how shaky the grounds are that Islamophobia is built upon.

Let's get this straight: it's not our fault that we can't speak English. It's because our husbands, fathers and brothers are chauvinists from foreign lands who think we might unshackle ourselves from the oven and start wearing hot pants if we learn how to tell the time in English. OK, got it. But at the same time, it *is* our fault that our sons are falling victim to radicalisation online because if we can't speak English, we can't tackle the threat from ISIS to young Muslim men. So we are both innocent and guilty. Meek, oppressed, silent and yet at the same time blameworthy, dangerous agents of terror at the dinner table. We must integrate into British society, but if we can't, for example, get a job because of institutional racism, access education because of poverty or get support because cuts have decimated any help we could have relied upon then we… might have to leave. No integration for you – you had your chance.

The only time Muslim mothers matter to the British state, and to society at large, is under the guise of counter terror. We do not matter when our mental health struggles are specific and unique, coloured by inherited cultural norms or the impact of being hyperpoliced in the place we call home. We do not matter when we face additional barriers to participation – like higher rates of poverty or lower rates of employment due to structural Islamophobia. We do not matter when our race affects the likelihood of us or our babies dying during labour or if our immigration status puts us in dangerous and precarious situations. We do not matter when we speak up about how programmes like Prevent surveil, police and infringe the rights of our families rather than safeguard them – how our children aren't free to make spelling mistakes at school or openly share their religious identities without being at risk of law enforcement. We are invisible when it's expedient and then worthy of millions of pounds of funding when it means laying the blame for state failings at our door or further criminalising us, our children and our communities.

I suppose, in many ways, the invisibility of motherhood is fleeting – coming in ebbs and flows through the seasons of our lives. I am able to go to work, to the supermarket and for a coffee on my own now without my son, a buggy or a baby sling on my person. He no longer thinks we are part of the same being; he's physically capable of living separate from my body now. I can exist as my own entity – even if the marks of my mothering will always remain.

When I returned to work after maternity leave, I soon figured out that I can – no, I must – navigate the world as though there isn't a part of my soul doing messy play in nursery somewhere with people who are not me. If society hates anything more than an overtly motherly mother in public wafting her baby in your face with wet wipes, nappies and fifty different child-related contraptions in tow, it's a woman who talks about being a mother constantly. Society soon teaches you the lesson that the baby you were conditioned to long for since childhood now needs to be practically a secret if you want to have any success back at work. But there's a word for it. Microchimerism. The transfer of cells between mother and baby during pregnancy. It's not possible to remove myself from someone whose DNA is forever entwined with my own.

And, paradoxically, I could very easily remove my hijab. On the surface, it's just a piece of cloth after all. I know if I was to simply remove it, I could become visible once more, too. I could slip under the barriers of racism, hop over the walls that Islamophobia has built in my life. My name, my accent and my mixed heritage could let me pass, even if just for a while, as someone who people see for once. I could get that flat white in Gail's without someone pushing in front of me and I could make friends with those mothers who look past me whilst our children make friends. But, of course, like microchimerism, there is something that cannot be extracted, unravelled. Like standing up to a possessive lover, if Britain doesn't accept *this* me, do I want its embrace at all?

That's the price of our invisibility – both as mothers and as invisible-hypervisible Muslim women wearing the hijab. It's as if society says acceptance and normality is within reach – just succumb, just acquiesce, just submit. Just work like you don't have kids so as not to inconvenience everyone else with things like sick days, sleepless nights and school plays. Just pretend it's normal to spend every waking second with someone glued to your skin for a year and then leave them with strangers for eight hours a day, five days a week. Just remove that hijab and integrate with Britishness, with whiteness. Don't burden us with your wanton Muslimness – your overt foreignness. We can make you seen again, but you have to meet us halfway. So easy, so tempting that can sound. But all that tells me is that Britain is a nation that offers acceptance and inclusivity only to those who fit its narrow definitions to begin with.

All the ways in which being visibly Muslim in Britain has shaped me, battered and bruised me into a different version of myself, has no doubt influenced what kind of mother I'll be, too. What kind of mother I already am. In this gentle-parenting, self-reflective era of motherhood that we – or at least the internet – find ourselves in, there's a lot of emphasis put on healing your own inner child so you don't perpetuate whatever traumas, whatever deep-rooted insecurities your own childhood imbued you with.

When my husband and I found out we were expecting a child, I already knew it was a boy and told everyone so because I was convinced I already had some kind of motherly intuition – and maybe I did – but regardless, I became obsessed with the name Zakaria. I even used to call him that – *Zakaria is kicking! We need to set up Zakaria's cot. Zakaria does a little loop-the-loop every time I eat chocolate!* (He – although no longer called Zakaria – is indeed a chocoholic, so I was right about that.) The name Zakaria was doing the rounds amongst European and American Muslims at the time. Every hijabi mumfluencer seemed to have a little Zakaria of her own, just like half a decade ago everybody had a little Noah. The feminine versions of these names are things like Alaia and Amaliah – ambiguous, exotic and blossoming with so many extra vowels that you can't quite tell what's beneath.

The baby name debate is always a contentious one, but my own obsession with the name Zakaria led me to unpack why I loved it so much and what function I really saw my child's name playing in the first place. Zakaria is the name of a prophet in Islam (and the other Abrahamic faiths) and when said in the proper Arabic, it drips melodically off the tongue. But, like my own name, it is also ethnically and religiously vague. A Zak (and, let's be real, he would become Zak) could be anything or anyone – and whilst that promises a lot of freedom, maybe would have secured him even a partial get-out-of-Islamophobia-free card, is that the message I want to be perpetuating in the next generation, in my own children?

Nobody wants to saddle their child with discrimination from birth, but the more I thought about it, the more my unborn child's name became a bigger question of purpose for me. What has this all been for? What has Muslimifying myself in the eyes of the public with a hijab on my head, abandoning the access to whiteness I could have otherwise had, all been for if I don't embed that sense of pride, that sense of reclaiming our identity, that sense of being unapologetic in our Muslimness in my own child?

But, really, it's more than just the name. And being called Zakaria, Nadeine, Adam or Mariah isn't what matters, really – and neither are people who choose those names for their children somehow doing something wrong. But becoming a mother has meant I've had to unpack and reevaluate how I am teaching my own child to be not just Muslim, and not just British, but British Muslim – an identity that I barely feel comfortable with myself. How can I teach him to be confident and unapologetic when I still feel like I have to seek permission to be in certain spaces? If I get nervous when I take him to a play area and all the other mums are white? If he grows up seeing me code-switch, watching me fold myself up to fit into whichever prescribed boxes the context requires, how will he ever know that he can be everything he is, all at once, all the time? That Britain should and must accept him regardless, because he is British regardless of what that Britishness looks like.

CHAPTER 7

MUSLIM MASCULINITY

ANDREW TATE, MINCELS AND THE AKH-RIGHT

'I'm gonna find myself a nice Islamic-ass wife. I'm gonna build up a big pile of rocks in case she gets fresh. I'm going to be prepared. So I ain't gonna mess around – as soon as I catch her cheating, there's gonna be no delays. In sha Allah.'

These are not the words of a misogynist reprobate lingering in the murkiest depths of Reddit, spewing hate about women whilst living off the goodwill of his mother. These are the words of Andrew Tate, reviled and revered TikTok megastar with millions of followers, talking about how the idea of being able to stone his non-existent Muslim wife for infidelity is one of the things that attracted him to Islam. Alarmingly, one in four young men in Britain agree with his views on women.

Tate's conversion to Islam may not have invented the

presence of misogyny within Muslim communities, but his newfound Muslim persona, the public reaction to it and even the atmosphere that produced it have arguably changed the landscape of British Muslimness for an entire generation – and possibly more.

Like any good influencer, Tate galvanised support for his journey to Islam right from the start. For months, he postured about Muslimness, flirting with Islamic ideas and stoking the support, and perhaps testing the waters, of a new, untapped follower base: young Muslim men. He posted ambiguous tweets referring to Qur'anic verses or Islamic aphorisms alongside his characteristic images of half-naked bodies, cigars and alcohol bottles. He appeared on the podcasts and YouTube channels of prominent (and often controversial) Muslim speakers and influencers, debating topics like the decline of Christianity, the nature of God, gender roles and 'the matrix'. He began referring to Islam as the 'last true religion in the world' and went to Muslim countries and met scholars who wrote nudge-nudge captions about brother Tate being close to finding the light.

Tate was already popular amongst boys and men who idolised his distilled view of masculinity as wealthy, desirable, dominating and successful. But, suddenly, it felt like every day – every hour – social media was flooded with young Muslim men praying for Tate to become Muslim, making dua (supplication) for him to find the right path and speculating about whether his heart had already accepted Islam. Us Muslims are always excited by the prospect of someone accepting the path that we believe to be the truth, but it felt like when it came to Tate, more was at play: like a generation of boys was desperate to see this tempting notion of masculinity sanctioned as being Islamic despite so much of it being totally antithetical to what our religion teaches. And as a Muslim woman, this was terrifying and infuriating to behold. I remember reading posts from other Muslim women expressing things like if Tate and everything he espouses can find convergence in Islam, what does that say about our faith? Or, even more extremely, that the notion of Tate being a Muslim would make them feel differently about their own faith identity altogether.

I think it's important to separate Islam from Muslims, my faith from my fellow believers. Whilst I believe Islam to be a perfect way of life, Muslims are flawed human beings who bring their own baggage, their own prejudices, their own inadequacies to the way we practise what we believe God has ordained. My concern with Tate accepting Islam wasn't because it would somehow change the fundamentals of how I understood my religion but because of what it would mean for Muslim women and men alike to have his hypersexualised, violent, dehumanising misogyny sanctioned as somehow Islamic. Maybe it's because I already saw how boys venerated him in the classroom, but the possibility of him being forever associated with Muslimness just seemed like atrocious PR – for our young boys as much as for the wider public perception of Islam.

Then, in 2022, Andrew Tate became a Muslim and it felt like a gaping chasm opened between Muslim men and women of my generation – or at least on so-called Muslim Twitter. I suppose that by nature of the echo chambers we form online, we surround ourselves with the same voices over and over again, but it felt like every time I went online, I was met with the same thing: posts from Muslim men celebrating Tate's conversion and even lauding him as a beacon of truth and light like a new-age religious guide, and Muslim women pointing out that he didn't seem to have stopped posting bikini-clad women, alcohol bottles or strange references to himself as some sort of deity, or that his human trafficking and rape accusations (at the time not yet charged) were still very real despite his recent cloak of Muslimness. And then the cycle would continue. Muslim men would urge us to make excuses for our new brother in faith, that his sins have been wiped clean now that he has accepted Islam and that we should be pleased for anyone entering our religion, regardless of what we think of them. And then Muslim women would argue that crimes of human trafficking or sexual assault are not wiped clean the same way that white lies might be, questioning why more excuses and patience are being offered for an alleged human rights abuser than they are for a Muslim woman who shows a strand of hair online. And then, invariably, the spat would end with the woman being called a 'feminazi' or some similar insult designed to diminish her points as being nothing but the brainwashing of liberal feminism.

As a Muslim woman during this time, it felt as though the men around us were falling into Tateism like flies. Scholars who Muslims of my generation had learned our religion from online as impressionable teenagers suddenly expressed their support for the viral influencer, even mocking Muslim women's concerns as nothing but the 'barking' of feminists. Typical derogatory descriptors used to dismiss Muslim women like the word 'bint' – which literally translates to 'girl' in Arabic but has come to mean a cross between a bimbo and a liberal feminist in the online Muslim lexicon – were being bandied about even by Muslims with major platforms. A section of the internet that had once felt like a safe space for Muslims to express and discuss our faith identity – especially when so much of real life disenfranchises us from being able to do this – turned into a place of hostility and even danger.

Inane 'debates' occupied the timeline every day, inevitably spurred by some ridiculous tweet from a young man barely through puberty, emboldened by this Tate-esque strain of Muslim masculinity that sees women as nothing but objects for male purpose and pleasure. Tweets about divorcing on the spot 'if my wife doesn't let me consummate within the first hour of marriage'. Posts advocating for virginity checks on a woman before marrying her – the assumption, of course, being that all Muslim women today are sexually promiscuous. Or suggesting young men go 'back home' and marry a (often teenage) girl from 'the village' who is untouched by feminism and knows nothing but obedience. Tweets comparing women who go to university and 'free mix' with men (e.g. sit within ten metres of them in a lecture hall) to OnlyFans influencers – and declaring that any father who lets his daughter attend higher education might as well just open her an account on the online pornography site and be done with it. Weird memes that anyone who has ever been in a real workplace for more than thirty seconds could tell you are inaccurate, in which women are depicted as saying no to making their husbands a cup of coffee (because they want a career) only to go and make a cup of coffee every five minutes for their boss. Endless, senseless drivel spurred by men postulating about what they'll do to their non-existent wives if they don't cook dinner, are secretly feminists, want to remove their hijabs or don't massage their mother-in-law's feet every ten seconds. Every post, every like, every share was as though our humanity was a football being kicked about for the entertainment of men set on manufacturing our suffering.

Misogyny, of course, has always existed within Muslim communities – like it has everywhere. For as long as men and women have been alive there have been structures of patriarchy to favour one and subjugate the other. But Tate's conversion marked a change that felt like a tidal wave. Perhaps it felt so devastating, so vulnerable to be a Muslim woman at that time because so much of what Tate espouses is so completely antithetical to Islam. Many Muslim women, myself included, cannot reconcile Tate's dehumanising, violent strain of misogyny with Islam's focus on ethics, social justice, equity and charity. How can an alleged human trafficker and rapist think his views are reflected in a religion that sought to provide rights to women where none existed before?

After all, whilst Europe was still debating whether women had souls and functioning brains, Islam came to liberate women in the ancient Arab world, affording women many of the rights that western societies still deprive us of today. Muslim women have the right to keep their own name after marriage and to retain their own property and money without being obliged to share it with their husband. Upon agreeing to get married, women are given a *mahr*, a sum of money decided mutually between both parties for the woman to do with as she pleases. Islam came to put an end to the atrocious practice of female infanticide practised by the pre-Islamic Arabs (and still prevalent in some parts of the world today) and forbade misogynistic acts like forced marriage or a woman being 'inherited' as a wife once her husband died. It is incongruous that a man who believes women to be sex objects can somehow come to represent masculinity for a faith community which believes in empowering and protecting women.

Whereas Tate prefers to call us hoes and bitches, Islam venerates women. Heaven lies under our mothers' feet, a promise that radically acknowledges the insurmountably hard job of being a mother – something that so-called progressive western societies still overlook today. Whilst Tate dismisses women as 'barely sentient', Allah orders believing men *and women* to read, to study, to ponder the nature of the universe because we are people in our own right with functioning brains, too. Tate talks about dating young women because they are easier to 'imprint' and how true masculinity is tied to sexual conquest, whereas Islam enshrines rights for women in a marriage to make sure they are never mere objects of satisfaction and abuse. In fact, the Islamic marriage contract itself secures us financial stability so that our husbands cannot exploit us or neglect our God-given rights.

Looking back now, I wonder whether Tate's conversion to Islam caused such a ripple of anger and confusion amongst many Muslim women because it signified a shift in the gender dynamics between men and women in our communities. Islam is often accused of favouring men, but, in reality, it grants men a significant responsibility over women – not to establish dominance but to absolutely enshrine our rights. It's unfashionable in our modern liberal system to consider this, but the way to empower and protect women isn't to work to dismantle the immovable patriarchy that has interwoven itself into every aspect of our lives – because whilst waiting to reach that end goal, what is happening to women at the hands of men right now? Rather, it's to hold men to account. To subvert the patriarchal narrative from one of subjugation to one of responsibility. Muslim men, for example, are mandated to provide financially for their families. This isn't to negate the woman's right to a career but to recognise the value of some women's work that is so often ignored, like motherhood. If Muslim men are obliged by God to provide their families with their basic needs and even to upkeep the lifestyle their wife experienced in her family home before getting married, this automatically levels the dynamic from one of control to one of mutual support. Islam teaches boys to respect and protect women, which might seem foreign and even archaic to progressive mindsets but is certainly better than teaching boys to see their female peers as objects from childhood, which is exactly what Tate does.

Andrew Tate normalised the idea of men and women as enemies and shrouded it in a cloak of Muslimness. Even if there had always been Muslim men who viewed masculinity as intrinsically superior to femininity, I'd argue that although thinking that men are better than women is still problematic, it has far less potential to spur violence than viewing women as some sort of combatant in need of battering into their rightful place. Most Muslim women are familiar with the cultural (not religious) notion that a woman's job is to have babies and clean the kitchen. I'm sure the majority of us will have come across a social media post or a video doing the rounds on the aunties' and uncles' WhatsApp groups proving that men's brains are wired for leadership whereas women's are built to nurture. Many of us will have been told by a random lady in the community that we're going to be left on the shelf if we aren't married by twenty-five. These things are nothing new.

But with Andrew Tate's conversion came a specific loathing towards women, an inherent mistrust, a violent lust for absolute control that I had certainly never experienced as a Muslim woman before. There'd always be a scholar somewhere posting videos about how the best thing a woman can be is a mother or a wife, but now suddenly it felt like we had regressed thousands of years to pre-Islamic notions of women being barely more than insentient slaves.

Muslim influencers became embroiled in banal debates with each other, getting blood-ragingly angry about bizarre fictional scenarios like wives being unfaithful or not being virgins before marriage. Their YouTube streams were suddenly full of furious, all-capitalised, clickbait videos, each encapsulating some imagined wrong committed by women towards mankind as a whole: *EX-WIVES USING KIDS AS BAIT. SAVE YOUR WIVES FROM HIJABI INFLUENCERS. WHY YOU SHOULD SPY ON YOUR WIFE'S PHONE. HIJABI BOSS BABE GETS REALITY CHECK.*

Internet sheikhs (self-ordained and often with little Islamic formal education) were getting hundreds and thousands of retweets for posting accusations about Muslim women's character and chastity despite such a thing being a grave sin in Islam. It felt like living in an alternate dystopian universe rife with disinformation and bubbling over with ferocious hatred. Every day it was 'all hijabis in the west are thots' (sexually promiscuous women) or advising young men to check who a woman is following on Instagram before marriage, to not marry a woman if she's been to university or if she's over the age of twenty-one. It felt as though an entire cohort of Muslim men had revoked their God-prescribed duty to be providers and protectors of women and instead saw us as immoral, deceitful opponents. It was as if the status I know Islam gives us no longer carried any weight because Andrew Tate and his ilk had made it acceptable – desirable, even – to despise women even within the confines of Muslimness.

The ironic and alarming thing is that Muslim women hadn't changed. We weren't suddenly disguising promiscuity under the veil of religious observance. We weren't going to university to flirt with boys. We weren't hopping from one relationship to another or planning to find a husband so we could take all his money and then use his kids to emotionally blackmail him. Muslim women remained the same. It was Muslim men who changed – or so it seemed. I knew of friends who had been talking to potential suitors for a number of months and were on the brink of securing dates to get married when suddenly the men would change and say something that had come straight from the Andrew Tate playbook: referring to themselves as 'high-value men' or asking my friends to give up the careers they'd spent years nurturing. I knew of more than one woman who was already married and overnight her husband wanted to sell their house and move in with his parents because he suddenly thought that good Muslim wives should live with their in-laws, despite him never expressing this before. I knew of Muslim women whose husbands had suddenly become controlling and dismissive of them as human beings – utterly obsessed with the domination husbands should maintain over wives as men. Tateism and its incongruous, distorted conversion with Muslimness felt like a disease that more Muslim men were succumbing to every single day.

The reason Andrew Tate's strain of patriarchy is so very potent in its hatred of women – and the reason it is so attractive to many young, impressionable men – is because it appeals to what has come to be termed the 'incel'.

'Incel' is shorthand for 'involuntarily celibate' and refers to an online subculture of mostly white, heterosexual men unable to get a partner despite desiring one. Hence: they are celibate against their will. They are characterised by a deep-seated hatred of women and the belief that women owe them gratification simply by virtue of being men. This places women in the position of sexual objects and men as being able to access them whenever they please, therefore glorifying rape culture and violence against women, especially those perceived to be denying men what they believe they are entitled to. Incel communities are defined by their self-pity and loathing, jealousy and anger towards men deemed more successful and are often depicted as being unemployed, financially inactive, living with parents and even having white supremacist political leanings. In 2022, the Center for Countering Digital Hate found that more than half of incels support paedophilia. Increasingly, the subculture has become linked to extremism with a number of high-profile mass killings being perpetrated by self-identified incels or those who expressed such tendencies online. Currently, 1 per cent of referrals to the UK's counter-terrorism strategy Prevent are defined as being linked to incel ideology. This may sound insignificant, but in the year to March 2022, this amounted to seventy-seven referrals whereas the year before this number was zero – indicating that the incel is an alarming and growing threat to the entire western world.

What is incongruous is that despite many of his supporters being incels, Andrew Tate is not one himself. His platform revolves around him boasting about his sexual conquests and his escapades with women. He regularly posts photos of himself on luxury yachts surrounded by women in bikinis. He supposedly teaches men how to 'get' a woman – or a 'female', as he likes to call us – and links masculinity directly and unflinchingly with domination over, and being desirable to, women. Now, Tate is the kind of man incels would usually hate because he is everything they are not. Incel forums often refer to 'Chads' – every stereotypical high school's popular guy who can get any girl he wants. In their world, Tate is the ultimate Chad. They are the boys who watch on with envy and rage bubbling inside them.

If we are to get technical, Andrew Tate is an advocate of the 'red pill' strain of men's rights activism. The 'red pill', of course, refers to the iconic '90s film *The Matrix* and symbolises having your eyes open to the truth rather than being blinded by how 'the matrix' or the powers that be want you to view the world. Red pillers see themselves as exclusively conscious of the supposed reality of the world we live in, like feminism's agenda to eradicate traditional masculinity or society's vendetta against the white man. Unlike incels who resort to violent fantasies and online anguish to express their victimhood, red pillers delineate using fitness and gym culture to coax women into wanting to sleep with them. From the red pill point of view, a so-called beta male can – and must – become an alpha male in order to access women's bodies and become a 'true man'.

This is where the crossover with some online Muslim subcultures exists. Sometimes referred to as Mincels (Muslim incels) or the akh-right ('akh' being the Arabic equivalent of 'bro'), this group has the political conspiracy theories of red pill ideology alongside all the sexual frustration of incels – even though, unlike classic incels, their celibacy is religiously prescribed unless within marriage. And, of course, the overarching commonality between all of these ideologically distinct subcultures is their hatred and denigration of women – and that they see themselves as victims of feminism's aim to emasculate men.

Mincels are heavily influenced by patriarchal cultural norms that have no basis in Islam and yet get misconstrued as being somehow Islamic – like banning wives, sisters and daughters from education and work or assuming that all the housework must be done by a woman. Because they see the world through the lens of victimhood at the hands of feminists, they cling to elements of Muslimness that seem to push back against this. They become obsessed with Islam's allowance of four wives without acknowledging the very specific conditions this ruling was supposed to apply to. They channel their incel-esque frustration at not being sexually gratified into an infatuation with virgins in heaven – even getting into preposterous debates with women online about how the women they are promised in heaven are better than any woman on this earth because we are all inherently flawed and corrupted (or, rather, possess the inconvenience of brains and voices). They distort Islam's prescription of gender roles into a rod to beat women with, staging bizarrely specific fictional scenarios for their followers online about whether to let your wife or your mother sit in the front seat of your car, who you greet first when walking into the house or whose side you take in an argument between the two women. For the Mincel, the incel's deep-rooted feeling of inadequacy is reimagined in the Muslim context of marriage. Men who might feel angry that they are not yet married in their mid-to-late twenties, who have been rejected by women who – in their eyes – are shallow and want a husband with a better job or more money, resort to feeling like they are victims of feminism and women at large. They may even spread disinformation about how Muslim women only want to marry men over six foot or highly racialised hysteria about how Arab and Asian women only want black men these days, again sparking those incel-rooted insecurities that more conventionally successful men are stealing the women that they should have a birthright access to. They even lean into the normalisation of paedophilia within the incel community by venerating the idea of bringing over a (very young) wife from back home. Like incels, their concern is that she hasn't been 'ruined' by exposure to other men and that her childlike qualities make an obedient wife. Despite Islam's firm prohibition on forced and child marriage (the bride must consent to the union), they resort to paedophilic tendencies because the more docile and naive their partner is, the more 'alpha' they are able to feel – which is ultimately their end goal.

At the same time, though, Mincels (or the akh-right) borrow ideas from red pill ideology, because as much as they feel that they are victims of feminism, they are also heavily influenced by the experience of growing up disenfranchised as young Muslim men in an inherently Islamophobic world. Like all Muslims, they have absorbed what it means to be securitised and criminalised your entire life because of having a Muslim name or brown skin or expressing Islamic beliefs. The notion of the political elite hiding the truth is already part of their vernacular because, like with many minority communities, us Muslims have manifold real-life examples of when political agendas distort blatant realities. Take the western world's unwavering support of Israel despite the nation inflicting seventy-five years of occupation and ethnic cleansing upon the Palestinian people – and having flouted the Geneva Convention countless times. We saw that weapons of mass destruction were a smokescreen to legitimise the massacre of a million Iraqis because we had friends, family and reputable alternative news sources on the ground. We know that we are not extremists for believing in God, that our children are not terrorists-in-waiting for asking for somewhere to pray at school, that our religion is not oppressive and evil – despite the narrative that the media and politicians conspire to create. And so if your life is already packed with examples of being lied to and misled by the powers that be, it's barely a jump at all to buy into conspiracies about 'the matrix' controlling our world order or the last real victim being the heterosexual male.

And, thus, red pill ideology becomes almost a crutch: a reassurance. It is better, after all, if you can't get married because all women are conspiring with feminists rather than because of your own personal failings. It is less of a blow to be unemployed because heterosexual men are the only true persecuted group (and all the jobs are going to women or other minorities) rather than simply not being good enough. It is easier to blame your problems on the world conspiring against you rather than to bother to do any introspection.

On an ideological level, it might seem incongruous that young Muslim men who have felt the brunt of the right-wing preoccupation with policing Muslims would ever align themselves with a subculture steeped in racism, white supremacy and political conservatism. Are the two not polar opposites? But there's another reason young Muslim men (and even a very small minority of women) find union in these red pill and incel ideologies: the feeling that traditional and socially conservative values are being eroded in our modern, liberal society. That feeling that nobody can speak the truth any more – whether it's about not wanting your child to be taught sex education at five years old, believing Covid-19 was a hoax or calling for all the immigrants to be kicked out. Speaking *your* truth gets you cancelled: this is the conviction that spurs these groups to converge even if their other religious, social and political views are at loggerheads.

A significant portion of Andrew Tate's online persona revolves around him saying what others dare not utter. His current Twitter (or X) bio is: '5 x boosted, Xe/Xim, Vice/BBC, BLM, Democrat, Vegan, Just Stop Oil, Climate change! Biden 2024', which is clearly designed to mock just about every perceived left-wing group going. He regularly posts about how he is the only voice of truth battling against the matrix – how 'feminists', 'LGBT', 'liberals' and 'big pharma' all want him to disappear – establishing himself as the last bastion of reason against ideologies intent to disrupt our natural, traditional world order. A lot of this is ego inflation, of course, but some of his words ring true for minority groups who feel that their way of life is no longer sanctioned by our increasingly progressive society. Men who don't think women deserve to be equal to them. People who believe in conspiracy theories about the Covid-19 vaccine or about big pharma implanting microchips in us. Tate deliberately strokes their insecurities and implants himself as the only alternative.

Most Muslims who hold normative Islamic values – like modest dress and behaviour, a belief in the sanctity of marriage or in God making men and women distinct from one another – can relate to the feeling of being maligned for your morals in a liberal system which accepts all lifestyles except those considered *il*liberal (and Muslims perpetually are exactly that). Muslim parents who are opposed to the contents of their children's sex education curriculum are routinely painted as archaic extremists – and even often referred to Prevent to be forcibly deradicalised. Muslims who speak openly about Islam's defined but complementary gender roles can be ousted as backwards, misogynistic or even transphobic. Muslim women extolling physical modesty are seen as self-hating draconian sexists. For a society that congratulates itself for being so progressive, Britain is astonishingly hostile to many of the views held by most observers of any faith, but especially when those ideologies are categorised as Muslim.

In the face of politicians who are too concerned with winning votes, a media that is too wrapped up in peddling its own agenda and even Muslim figures who are so eager to get to the table that they'll sell their more traditional values on the way, Muslim communities can feel like there is nobody in the mainstream who genuinely represents their interests or viewpoints. Tate fills this vacuum, disguising the violent misogyny and trafficking allegations behind a puff of cigar smoke and a veil of pseudo-religiosity.

Like any good businessperson, Tate knows his market. He knows that Muslimness itself is punished in the west. It is in his (and his wallet's) interest to whip up a frenzy of support and even controversy around himself because in our algorithm-driven world, the more people who are talking about him, the more traction he is getting – and the bigger, and more lucrative, his platform becomes. Taking on the identity of a persecuted religion like Islam allows him to mask his vitriol in the politics of the marginalised. Any Muslim knows that we are disproportionately targeted in the UK (according to the Home Office, half of all hate crimes are aimed at Muslims), so by, for example, conveniently holding a Qur'an whilst being arrested in front of the world's cameras, Tate gets to shift some of the attention away from the shocking allegations made against him personally and instead blame it on Islamophobia, the 'matrix' or the west's rejection of Islam's traditional values. He wraps his venom up in a cloak of victimhood and drags along in his wake an entire generation of Muslim men who feel politically and ideologically disenfranchised and insecure about their own manhood. I can't speak to how genuine his conviction for Islam is in his heart, but it seems little coincidence that Tate's entry into Muslimness gave him, overnight, an entire cohort of impressionable men and boys looking for someone to follow. And Muslims are in such numbers worldwide that Tate granted himself a billion new potential followers in one fell swoop.

Tate establishes himself as a martyr of traditional masculinity and this strikes a chord with young Muslim men who also feel like their very identity as men and as Muslims is criminalised. Muslim history is full of figures who embody traditional masculine ideas. Men who fought for the right to be Muslims, resisted persecution and died in the way of

Allah. Muslim men are mandated to be heads of the family, to provide and to protect. However, we are experiencing a crisis of masculinity in our modern age which places impressionable boys in a dangerously vulnerable position. By lambasting toxic masculinity without providing young men with an alternative, by cutting youth provisions and in turn preventing boys from having a healthy and productive outlet, by hyperpolicing poor and black and brown boys on the street through stop and search and by failing to properly protect children exposed to violent pornography and graphic content online, we do a disservice to the next generation of men. And we propel them right into the laps of the likes of Andrew Tate.

At the same time, Muslim men are struggling to fulfil the very masculinity that they feel has been outlawed in the first place, because of the financial and social implications of Islamophobia in the UK. The British Muslim community is one of the most heavily affected by poverty, and Muslim men of certain ethnicities have some of the lowest rates of higher education, stable employment and social mobility in the whole country. So whilst they tie traditional masculinity to getting a good job, having desirable material possessions (like fast cars and a big house), getting married young and providing for their family, in reality this is nothing but a far-fetched notion for many who are kept poor and disenfranchised by impenetrable cycles of poverty and structural Islamophobia.

So if these traditional notions of what it means to be a 'man' are harder to access, more extreme (and more terminally online) versions of masculinity become appealing. Even if they have very little to do with the faith system that fuels your search for true masculinity in the first place. Tate steps in to sell these vulnerable, impressionable and often dejected young men the idea that women and feminism are to blame for all their problems, that they deserve a beautiful, passive woman just because they're a man. That women only want men who are muscular, powerful and rich. Oh, and that the secret to becoming those things is all here in this exclusive online programme that will cost you hundreds of pounds to enrol into...

Fundamentally, Islam doesn't really come into what Tate espouses because, by its nature, Islam is entirely opposed to everything he says. Tate is all black and white, leaving no room for the nuance of grey. Muslim men might see in him a reflection of Muslim masculinity as it 'should' be, but what is overlooked is that Islam also has ample examples of Muslim men embodying a more gentle side, too, like how the Prophet Muhammad (peace be upon him) mended his own clothes by hand, helped with the housework and was a loving, doting father and husband. But in the warped, polarised conceptualisation of gender roles that Tate relies upon to stay relevant, these characteristics are dismissed as feminine. Tate isn't interested in representing a comprehensive, complex Muslim masculinity. Take a look at any of his content and the double standards are glaringly obvious – posing half-naked next to women in bikinis, openly drinking alcohol and smoking cigars in the middle of Ramadan and referring to himself as some kind of godlike deity to be worshipped – none of these hint at genuine piety nor the Muslim values that define our faith. But somehow that doesn't matter because Tate represents a revival of the dying breed of the True Man to men desperately trying to understand their own identities. Tate borrows the language of faith, lubricating his harsh ideas into something more palatable to his largely religious audience, but he establishes himself – rather than Allah – as the actual deity at the centre.

He is the one to be followed. It dwindles into irrelevance that his entire platform is a business rather than innocent philanthropic advice from an older brother. His vile misogyny, the shame he creates in his male fanbase and the sprinkle of religion he decides to add every couple of weeks are carefully constructed elements of the same overall aim: to sell. And that he does. For a mere $8,000, you can join 'a global network in which exemplars of individualism work to free the modern man from socially induced incarceration' (whatever that means), or for $50 a month, you can subscribe to his online Hustler's University, which promises to teach men how to make money and become an 'alpha male' – including, alarmingly, those under eighteen who are encouraged to join and 'pull in thousands a month'. The glaring irony that Tate's platform feeds off of men desiring to be like him but never achieving his self-professed lofty heights of masculinity falls by the wayside entirely, because he is creating the perfect conditions for a storm that we will see the repercussions of for years to come: a new generation of young men whipped up in a frenzy of inceldom validated by distorted religious justifications, self-esteem issues and a brimming hatred for women. And he will be the one raking in the profits, at the cost of the safety of women and the future prospects of impressionable young boys.

At the same time, it is crucial we ask ourselves that in our Islamophobic system, which versions of Muslim masculinity are the ones that are allowed to proliferate? Which are the ones, whether directly or indirectly, facilitated by the structures that ordain our lives?

Ultimately, there is no conceptualisation of the Muslim man that is acceptable to the western palate – unless it is one that is devoid of its Muslimness entirely. Muslim men who espouse stereotypically chivalrous behaviour – the type that has us doe-eyed at Disney princes – are seen as misogynistic. Muslim men who embody physical strength – like Palestinians resisting Israeli occupation, Iraqis defending themselves against western invasion or North Africans revolting against their dictators – are portrayed as barbarians and exceptional in their violence. Muslim men who have risen to mainstream positions of influence or power in the western sphere are forced to shirk their Muslimness entirely. Muslim politicians whitewash themselves; Muslim athletes tread careful lines when discussing religious or political views in public and are punished if those views don't match the dominant narratives of the west. Even peripheral Muslim male characters on our TV screens are sanitised with a white wife or a job in the police force – unless, of course, they are a villain, in which case their Muslimness will be centre stage and the very reason for their cruelty and misogyny.

This is no surprise. The liberal west exists for its own colonial ends. When (white) Ukrainian men stayed behind to defend their homes and cities from invading Russian forces, they were lauded as brave freedom fighters and legitimate heroes. News segments and documentaries, politicians' speeches and international aid organisations all dedicated their attention to the courage and valiance of these men who had sent their women and children to safety whilst putting their own lives on the line. When British men join the army and engage in violence overseas, including the murder of civilians, they are considered to be the definition of bravery. They are cast as *protecting our nation* (although we are rarely told from what). When it's white men in question then bloodlust, strength and brutality are considered admirable traits, deserving of moments of silence and remembrance days, poppies and entire charities in their name.

But there is no alternative for Muslim men – not one that is remotely positive anyway. If white colonial forces (like the British Army) are the good guys, by default those on the other side (almost always Muslims) are the bad guys. Unlike Ukrainians, when Muslim men defend their homes, families and lands from occupiers, they are rebels and terrorists, savages and thugs. It doesn't matter if that same pursuit was noble when it was white hands making Molotov cocktails instead of brown hands throwing rocks, because the west needs us to see Muslim men as scarcely more than feral beasts in order to legitimise their slaughter at the hands of its own liberal, colonial pursuits.

This has never rung more true than right now, as Israel carpet-bombs Gaza in what it and the entire western world sanctions as self-defence. As seventy-five years of occupation, ethnic cleansing and displacement culminates in a final genocide of the population of Gaza (half of whose population are children), the media has instead been fixated on peddling narratives of Palestinian men as terrorists and barbarians. As soon as events escalated, the news wasted no time in perpetuating Islamophobic propaganda about Palestinians beheading babies and raping women despite there being no evidence to support these claims. Every paper ran headlines about forty babies being beheaded by Palestinian groups before there was even any photographic backing to these claims. In fact, Joe Biden stood on a world stage and said he had seen images of these beheaded babies despite Israel itself later confirming that no such evidence existed. But it didn't matter that there weren't forty beheaded babies. It didn't matter that one female hostage shook the hands of Hamas representatives when she was released, or that she said the first thing the hostages were told was 'we are Muslims and we will not hurt you'. Nobody cares because everybody (the media, our politicians, society at large) is too busy salivating at the portrayal of Muslim men as the uncivilised terrorists we've always been told they are.

Meanwhile, footage from Gaza shows a depiction of Muslim masculinity that disproves everything the world has been told about Muslim men. Palestinian men are pulling babies out of rubble with their bare hands. Climbing into precarious, dilapidated infrastructure to follow the faraway screams of someone trapped underneath. They are operating on civilians with no anaesthetic and under torchlight, being called to identify the bodies of their own families and then returning to operate through the night. They are livestreaming the devastation for the whole world to see even if it means risking their own life doing it. They are fasting so their families can eat the sparse food available, taking in newly orphaned children whose entire bloodline was wiped out in an instant and picking up the pieces of their children's obliterated bodies in plastic bags. They are dressing up as Mickey Mouse to cheer people up and writing love poetry on the shrouds of their wives' bodies, covering the shattered faces of their infants so nobody else has to witness what they just have and taking the time to comb their daughters' hair before they are buried in a mass grave. All whilst having a camera thrust in their face because that's the only way to prove their humanity to a world blind to it.

Yet, the west looks the other way because dehumanising Muslim men and portraying them as scheming terrorists deserving of the most brutal death is the only way to maintain the charade that its own colonial agendas are legitimate. That they are the good guys. Even aid organisations or governments that are more sympathetic will speak only of the 'innocent women and children of Gaza', criminalising and condemning all Palestinian men in one go. Brown Muslim men who embody the same strength we venerate in white men are barely even granted the luxury of living, let alone being celebrated or seen as human.

We have to ask ourselves why this noble, honourable, selfless strain of Muslim masculinity is erased and securitised, and yet the media will be very quick to show a young Muslim boy who has been radicalised or focus on a murderer's faith background if they happen to be Muslim. I'm not going to give a free pass to misogynists who twist Islam into a weapon to curb women's freedoms. But at the same time, I'm not about to feed into the convenient narratives that our Islamophobic leaders want us to swallow either. Mincels are useful for a government that survives on the dehumanisation of Muslims. They fit all the prescribed stereotypes. Misogyny? Check. Thirst for violence? Check. Feelings of disenfranchisement? Check. The existence of Mincels – and seeing all Muslim men as a variation of this ideology – allows the government to legitimise the broadening of Prevent, sanction its aggressive foreign policy and validate its policing of the entire Muslim community.

Much like the Muslim woman, whatever the Muslim man does, he is wrong. If he defends himself, he is a terrorist. If he is sucked into viral online trends, he is a Mincel. Yet, if we look at the conditions that have created this wave of Minceldom (or akh-right ideology) at its root, it is clear that many are manufactured politically, socially and economically by those in power: the very people who are so eager to condemn Muslim masculinity for being inherently patriarchal in the first place.

When Prevent was first established under Tony Blair's Labour government, it focused on giving funding to community groups to tackle community disenfranchisement and radicalisation on the ground. Its aims were neoliberal in nature, blaming Muslim communities for their own problems. It conflated female equality with this aim and funded groups that promoted girls' education, women's participation in civic life and campaigning against child or forced marriage because it inaccurately linked radicalisation to the disenfranchisement of women rather than bothering to interrogate why Muslim women are barred from access in the first place. Its approach to women was problematic enough, but its focus on men crystallised the lens of criminalisation and surveillance that still prevails today. MI5 paid Muslim men to become spies on their communities and within their mosques. Surveillance cameras were placed in Muslim suburbs in cities such as Birmingham to survey the comings and goings of (mostly) Muslim men. Spaces frequented by Muslim men during Jumuah (Friday prayer) or Taraweeh (night prayers) during Ramadan were – and still are – targeted for surveillance.

At the same time, with the dawn of austerity, we saw debilitating cuts to vital services: youth centres and clubs, schools and mental health support. Most Muslims live in the most deprived areas of the UK, the very same regions hit the hardest by austerity policies. Muslim boys of some ethnicities have some of the worst educational outcomes of any group. According to Census 2021 data, Muslims are the least likely group to be in a managerial position and the most likely to have no qualifications. If a society criminalises masculinity when it is associated with Muslimness, eradicates any structural support available to boys in the most disadvantaged areas and disenfranchises an entire demographic of the population through aggressive foreign policy and an increasingly Islamophobic domestic policy, it seems like only a matter of time before someone like Andrew Tate fills that tragically gaping chasm.

CHAPTER 8

A NATION WITHIN A NATION

HOW CLASS COMPOUNDS ISLAMOPHOBIA IN BRITAIN

I didn't know I was working class until I went to my best friend's house in secondary school and her fridge was full of things I'd never tasted before. Smoked salmon. Ben & Jerry's ice cream. Green & Black's chocolate and Tropicana juice. The ketchup and the beans were Heinz and the washing-up liquid was Fairy. The eggs were free range and the tuna was John West. The cupboards were a cornucopia of Waitrose.

Beyond being thrilled at the prospect of eating luxury coleslaw straight out of the tub every time I went to her house, I didn't think much about what this meant. I didn't realise this symbolised something bigger, deeper, about the difference between us and that those divisions ruled the entire world in which we were growing up.

Then I got to university. And straight away, everyone on my small course asked each other what school they went to when they first met, which I thought was odd until I realised it's because they all went to such renowned institutions that they recognised the names. They spoke about gap years in Goa, having just got back from backpacking in South America and holiday homes on the Continent. It smacked me in the face, this realisation of the class difference between us. But it wasn't just about their schools or how they spent their holidays. They basked, they marinated, they swooshed around dressed in more self-confidence than I had ever seen in my life, words and accents like velvet tumbling out of their mouths. At first I thought it was just whiteness – I was, after all, acutely aware of my own lack thereof every time I sat in a lecture theatre with the twelve or so students I was to be bound to for the next three years. But it was more than that. It was all the assertiveness and power of whiteness set ablaze with the burning privilege of wealth. I was seeing that up close for the first time in my life: the blinding credence that you belong here – that this space was constructed precisely for you – and it made me realise the opposite about myself. That I didn't belong and that these spaces weren't made for me at all, even if I had got the grades to be there. I was masquerading as something I wasn't, and I felt sure that the mask would slip off.

A couple of months after I started university, I met an old school friend at home. The first thing she said was that my accent had changed. I had subconsciously made myself sound more 'posh' to align myself with the voices I felt I had to compete with in every seminar room. I remember tripping over my words every time I was forced to speak. Swallowing the burning answers I wanted to give because I didn't want to speak in front of these people who had probably taken elocution lessons as children, or so I imagined. Every time I did speak, in those awkward moments waiting outside the classroom for the teacher to arrive, the eyes of my coursemates would gloss over and they'd quite literally look the other way; I could tell they weren't taking in anything I was saying. I suppose privilege recognises when it's not in its own company and looks for a way out. The one friend I did make on my course – one of the only other non-white students – dropped out after a couple of weeks. She said the rest of them made her feel stupid for her thick Coventry accent. Even now, I'm painfully aware that my accent is more the product of my own self-doubt in those three fleeting years of my life than it is of where I grew up. I can hear the tapestry of a Northampton accent overlapping with words that are excessively over-pronounced and, more recently, an east London twang.

Social class matters when thinking about Islamophobia and structural racisms more broadly because class signals proximity to power and the only source of that power in our society is often whiteness. Who gets that privilege – who gets to be an acceptable Muslim, an ideal migrant, palatable to this nation that forces out foreignness at its root – ultimately comes down to who gets to access whiteness. And the only way is to buy your way in.

Growing up, my dad was always adamant that Britain wasn't 'our home' – even if half of the blood that ran through my brother's and my veins was English. Even if our mother was white. What he meant, of course, was that it wasn't *his* home, despite his passport and thirty years here suggesting otherwise. As a child, this confused me. I wondered what it meant to not really be at home in the one place you've lived your entire life. I pondered, and feared, what it meant if my dad's home was not the same as my own. Would there come a day where we were all split up, forced to return to our true homes? And which would mine be?

At the time, I didn't recognise that my dad's mindset was a symptom of our class identity as a family – or that it was a coping mechanism for a lifetime of racial subjugation. I guess if you never allow yourself to feel at home, it doesn't hurt as much when that home reminds you that you don't belong after all. My dad worked all kinds of jobs, in warehouses and factories, driving buses, operating forklift trucks. I can see now what I couldn't see then: that when power is intertwined with whiteness, it's hard to comprehend a way to be an ethnic minority in a blue-collar or service industry without feeling like you're ultimately in servitude of the elite and the white. Whether we are driving their buses and taxis, cleaning their houses and offices, delivering their takeaways or nannying their children, our employment and therefore class status bind us in a position of inferiority which cannot help but affect how we view our place in this country. And if that place is already sitting on tenterhooks, forced into precarity by hostile politics and institutional racism, the result is that you see you don't belong in this country even if you do call it home.

Muslim communities have long been some of the most affected by poverty in the United Kingdom and this has become more acute recently due to the cost-of-living crisis. According to the 'Muslims and the Cost of Living Crisis' report conducted by Muslim Census in 2022, around half of all Muslims in Britain live in poverty compared to around 18 per cent of the general population. Muslims are far more likely to live in the most deprived urban areas and the numbers of Muslim individuals and families taking on debt to cover household bills far supersedes that of their non-Muslim counterparts. As found by Muslim Census, one in three Muslims in Britain misses one meal a day due to financial difficulty. During Ramadan 2023, the National Zakat Foundation reported that a Muslim requested to receive zakat (charity) once every twelve minutes. In 2022, it was once every thirty minutes.

The latest data from the standard United Kingdom census from 2021 cements the picture that, economically, things have rarely been worse for Muslims in Britain. Those who identified as Muslim were almost four times more likely to live in overcrowded homes than the general population and had the lowest number of people aged sixteen to sixty-four in employment. Muslim respondents were the least likely religious group to live in their own home and the most likely to live in social housing. And Muslims were more likely than the average UK population to work in so-called elementary occupations, defined as involving routine tasks or physical effort.

Not only are Muslims uniquely economically disenfranchised but structural Islamophobia aggravates this, further disadvantaging us as a community. According to a survey by Hyphen, a media platform that focuses on the voices of Muslims in the UK and Europe, seven in ten Muslims have experienced Islamophobia at work. This cannot be removed from the census finding that Muslims have the lowest representation in employment at managerial and senior levels. When racism forms an indestructible barrier to progression and higher wages, poverty becomes a given and social mobility a pipe dream. The reason this matters is because the reality of being poor in our class-ruled society binds us as Muslim communities in a state of instability and impermanence.

Think about the notion of the perfect immigrant. They are expected to assimilate fully, which means doing something exceptional like becoming the leading brain surgeon at a children's hospital or at the very least have the decency to get a high-paid job and go by a shortened version of their inconveniently foreign name. The perfect immigrant should speak impeccable English, preferably with an accent others have no problem understanding. They should never at any point in their lives rely upon the support of the state because they aren't really entitled to it anyway. And heaven forbid they express an opinion that doesn't toe the line of the government-mandated status quo.

This entire framework is not just one of racism; it is one of classism. The perfect immigrant is the rich immigrant. The privileged immigrant. The highly educated immigrant who comes from a wealthy family abroad and aligns themselves with right-wing politics once they're here – ironically – to stop people like them from coming into England ever again. The only ideal, perfect immigrant is one that is barely an immigrant at all. An Englishman in brown(ish) wrapping.

Dismantling class barriers is vital for demolishing Islamophobia because social class is so tightly woven into many factors – our immigration status, our employment situation, our education level and our housing security. It's difficult to engage in civic life when your priority is surviving to the next pay cheque. When your experience of reality is zero-hour contracts, homelessness and poverty, it's impossible to find time to grapple with questions of what it means to be British. Being unapologetic about our Muslimness, smashing stereotypes and subverting narratives are all far-flung luxuries when we're struggling to put food on the table.

The thing about poverty is that it shackles your entire existence. Everything comes down to getting by because you don't have the financial cushion of savings in the bank or the reassurance that you own the roof over your head. If your job is one that doesn't require a specific university degree or an advanced level of education, it can leave you feeling like you dare not rock the boat – don't bring up politics in the canteen, don't tell anyone you're fasting in Ramadan, don't grow that beard or wear that hijab in case you get fired for it. If the only snapshot of Britain you are ever allowed to see is one where assimilation looks like acquiescence and where keeping your job is more important than asserting your own identity, why are you going to risk the food on your family's table just to be unapologetic about who you are?

Muslims disengaging from politics has long been a growing fear, but until recently, it hasn't quite been a fully-fledged reality across the board. Generally, Muslims have lent their political support to the Labour Party – like many ethnic minority groups. Perhaps it's because the Conservatives remain tarnished by the legacy of the likes of Enoch Powell and the era of the 'If you want an N-word for a neighbour, vote Labour' line. Maybe it's because despite being socially conservative, Muslims tend to be more reliant upon a large and generous state, which the Conservatives are diametrically opposed to. Or perhaps, like in my case, it's just because Labour is the lesser of two evils (although the Iraq War and, more recently, Keir Starmer's sacking of anyone who supported a ceasefire in Gaza reinforces the fact that they both really are evils). Either way, Labour has long been the party of choice for Muslims – so much so that it has come to take us for granted.

But things are changing. A study conducted by Muslim Census in October 2023, which includes the views of around 30,000 British Muslims spread across nearly 580 constituencies, found that Muslim support for Labour has dropped by a sobering 66 per cent, indicating that only 5 per cent of Muslims intend to vote for Labour in the next election. In the majority of cases, the reason given is Keir Starmer's response to Israel's continued bombardment of Gaza, including his treatment of any MPs who call for a ceasefire and his repeated support for Israel's right to defend itself even when that entails carpet-bombing thousands of civilians. This is not surprising, given the overwhelming support for the Palestinian cause in the Muslim community. In fact, this collective Muslim disapproval for the sanctioning of genocide against our Palestinian siblings should be a reminder to all in parliamentary politics that us British Muslims are able to (and will) be more selective about who we allow to represent us in the future. It is no longer enough to offer us nothing more than, 'we're not as bad as them!' or hollow diversity that quietly, in the background, quashes all dissent of thought and beliefs. We will, and we are, demanding more.

However, the Muslim Census study also concluded something alarming. If there was an election tomorrow, 40 per cent of Muslims would not vote at all. If poverty prevents Muslims from participating in society, barring us from our political systems entirely, our voices fail to be included in policy-making and our criticisms whittle away into nothing, lost in whispered comments and WhatsApp groups. If Muslims don't vote, if we are too bound by our daily plight of feeding our children and paying rent to grapple with the policies that disenfranchise us in the first place, if we lack the mental space to organise against legislation like Prevent which criminalises our youth, we simply aren't heard as a community. And this allows dominant narratives, hostile politics and stereotypes presented as fact to go unchallenged. For all the valid criticisms of democracy (and there are many), any functioning, healthy, genuine democracy is built upon the participation of the people. And if an entire cohort of the population are disempowered from engaging at all, that means that we Muslims continue to be the subjects of policy without ever playing an active part in its creation – or at the very least holding to account the ruling class who are the ones doing the decision-making.

Perhaps depending on how much of a cynic you are, you might view the growing political disengagement of Muslims in Britain in a number of ways. Is it that our politicians have underestimated us? Assumed that our politics will remain static? Presumed us to be passive sheep following the crowd year upon year, generation after generation? It certainly seems as though certain politicians on the left – including the current Labour leader, Keir Starmer – have taken Muslim potential voters for fools. In October 2023, after peddling the line for the best part of two weeks that Israel has the right to defend itself, including by cutting off food, water and fuel to Gaza, Starmer trotted off to a mosque in Wales to tell the congregants not only that Hamas should release their Israeli hostages (as if they're being held in the basement of a Welsh mosque) but also that he didn't think Israel had the right to cut off those vital supplies after all. Either politicians think we British Muslims have very short memories, that we don't engage enough with politics in the first place to smell a barefaced lie when it's in front of our noses, or they wrongly think we are so unmoved by the decades of occupation and ethnic cleansing of our counterparts in faith that we are unbothered by a former human rights lawyer defending war crimes that flout the Geneva Convention and then denying that very act in our place of worship.

Still, it could be the case that politicians simply have their sights set elsewhere. Muslimness may be a cloak that certain politicians don or flirt with in order to get into power (think Sajid Javid referring to his Muslim heritage when it suits him and calling himself a Christian at other times) or that political parties flex to show off their diversity, but there is little appetite for actually representing our views, our grievances and our demands beyond sticking a couple of brown faces in the Cabinet. After all, as a community, we don't have the wealth, status and connections of other demographics. Why should a political system predicated on personal gain be interested in our voices? As the entire nation jolts right – and the government to boot – it seems less likely that politicians will run after the vote of a mere 6.5 per cent of the general population when there's power and success to be found in an increasingly mainstream dog-whistle politics that is set on demonising us instead. It's no coincidence that as Muslims continue to disengage organically, we are at the same time being ever-more iced out of parliamentary politics altogether.

But I suppose I am more cynical than that, because if I have learned anything about being Muslim in Britain, it's to always presume the worst and you'll usually find evidence to support that hypothesis. Could the political disenfranchisement of Muslim communities be an end goal of Islamophobia by design? Built into our liberal system itself? Our nation exists for its own colonial agendas; we live in a liberal system which seeks to brainwash and manipulate the narratives so that certain voices and lifestyles are demonised and others are upheld as the pinnacle of liberalism. Muslim voices are dangerous to an agenda that intends to murder us abroad and subjugate us at home. And whether directly or indirectly, shutting off our recourse to legitimate democratic engagement means that our governments can act with impunity. They can sanction genocide of our siblings in faith abroad. They can create the most dystopian racist policies domestically – like shipping migrants off to Rwanda or holding them on a prison ship at sea (both policies that have been found to disproportionately affect Muslim migrants, by the way). They can create the perfect conditions for our so-called radicalisation (disenfranchisement, poverty, untreated mental illness, aggressive foreign policies, criminalisation of Muslimness at home) and then punish us when we fall into the trap – policing and securitising our children for having political opinions, rendering us extremists for calling out Islamophobia and terrorists for siding with the plight of Muslims abroad. They can remove our citizenship if we don't acquiesce, making us someone else's problem even if all we have displayed is what we are taught at school to be British values: standing up for the rule of law, freedom of speech and freedom of belief.

Increasingly, every effort is being made to bar Muslims from legal, peaceful forms of political resistance or expression. Accusations of antisemitism, extremism, opposing 'British values' or even supporting terrorism are waged against us in order to demobilise and disempower us, in order to stifle our voices. Legal and social frameworks are put in place in order to quash our views and by extension any criticism of the state. Write a social media post in support of innocent people not being massacred in Palestine and your employer will sack you for antisemitism. Wear a Palestinian pin badge to school and your teacher will assume you're an extremist and refer you to Prevent. Openly criticise Prevent and that, ironically, is a signifier of extremism, so you'll be, you got it, referred to Prevent. Even Muslimness itself is politicised unless we succumb to the state's pressure to push our religious identity to the sidelines and view Britishness as our only true persona. In the 2023 review of the Prevent duty, the term 'Islamism' is problematically defined as when one's Islam forms the centre of their identity and everything is informed by that religious conviction, which sounds like every practising Muslim since the dawn of our faith.

Being peaceful is not enough to quell the public and political appetite to criminalise Muslims at every turn, rendering our every opinion extreme and contrary to British society. The BDS (Boycott, Divestment and Sanctions) movement is a campaign to apply pressure to Israel to comply with international law by, in part, boycotting companies that operate in occupied Palestinian territories. Though not a Muslim movement, it has become racialised as a perceived Muslim grievance and, more crucially, as 'antisemitic' despite various university student unions and institutions complying with BDS and major Jewish voices supporting its aims. At the time of writing, a bill has just been passed in the UK Parliament that outlaws public bodies' right to boycott companies based on foreign policy – and the legislation specifically establishes Israel as one of the nations whose produce it will become illegal to boycott. When it was being debated in the House of Commons, words like Hamas, antisemitism and extremism were bandied about as though to imply that even *refraining* from doing something (in this case being a public body that buys Israeli products) is something to be criminalised, policed and curbed. Though aimed at public bodies, legislation such as this creates the deliberate and convenient misconception that *all* boycotting of Israeli goods is unacceptable, antisemitic and now illegal – by proxy criminalising what is standard Muslim political expression.

The chilling move to increasingly delegitimise and outlaw the right to protest must be seen as part of this selfsame programme of Islamophobia, too, of disarming the Muslim community at large. Throughout the autumn of 2023, hundreds of thousands of people flocked to central London to protest against the ongoing assault on Gaza and hold our western politicians to account for aiding and abetting Israel's war crimes. The then Home Secretary and our Prime Minister have pushed the narrative that these are 'hate marches', that they are antisemitic and that they glorify terrorism. Sections of the tabloid media have framed them as 'jihadi gatherings', deliberately plastering highly racialised pictures on their front pages – like men with big beards chanting about the freedom of Palestine or women in niqabs holding banners calling out the Israeli state – to create an association between visible Muslimness and political extremism. Before she was sacked as Home Secretary, Suella Braverman hinted that waving the Palestinian flag could be seen as supporting terrorism. The police use tactics to intimidate and curb the legal right to protest, including harassing people for having Palestinian flags on their cars and homes and accusing anyone of showing visible support for Palestine as stoking community tensions. The latest in this string of hypocrisy and flagrant Islamophobia is the line the government peddled about Armistice Day, that holding a pro-Palestine march would 'desecrate' the 'sanctity' of the day – serving us with a reminder that peace was never meant for us, that some lives deserve a ceasefire and some don't, that calling for an end to the genocide of Muslims and Arabs is vehemently opposed to British values (exposing all we needed to know about the integrity of those so-called British values in the first place). The fact that after all the hysteria, it was, ironically, far-right protesters igniting violence by 'defending' the Cenotaph from the jihadis they had been primed by our government and media to expect barely seemed to matter at all in the end because the political arrow had hit its mark. Palestine supporter equals terrorist (and therefore non-British).

Muslim voters are disenfranchised from political involvement not only through manufactured conditions of poverty but also through ostracising us with blatantly Islamophobic political stances, like blanket support for Israel and firing anyone in your party who disagrees. At the same time, our legal right to express our political viewpoints in other ways, through protest and boycotting, is criminalised. We are pushed to a position of feeling censored, impotent and bubbling over in frustration by the very same public and the very same elite that then wastes no time in revelling in that anger when it surfaces, pointing at us and saying, 'See! We told you they were barbarians! Get them out!'

It's no coincidence that when Muslims do climb the class hierarchies that divide and rule Britain, they often have to leave their visible Muslimness at the door. Our highest-ranking Muslim representatives in government often sanitise their image by being less *overtly* Muslim, maybe not wearing a hijab or not having a beard. Having a white spouse. A child in the army. Muslim politicians who co-opt their faith identity in order to win the votes of the demographics they claim to represent are then struck with the cruel paradox that they would never have got to that position if they actually offered anything radical that centres around faith or offers a platform to the voices of the Muslim community. Somewhere on the road to status and influence, visible Muslimness has to get left behind because this nation requires us to stay in positions of subjugation in order to keep us contained, to keep us in our place.

The trouble is, it's not just that economic hardship pushes Muslim communities out of political discourse, disengaging us entirely from civic life. There's also the fact that symptoms of poverty themselves are criminalised when expressed by Muslims, especially children and young adults. The Prevent duty incumbent on all public sector workers identifies factors like increasing levels of anger, becoming withdrawn, going through a personal crisis, struggling with a need for belonging and becoming obsessed with a desire for the system to change as possible signs that a person is being radicalised into extremist ideology. Now, you tell me what young person who is battling homelessness, who is looking after baby siblings whilst their parents are working back-to-back shifts, who can't afford basic food, hygiene products or school supplies, isn't going to feel those things? The list of suspicious behaviours reads like an inventory of very normal responses to being a child living in severe financial hardship. Even mental illness, which has a direct correlation with poverty, is twisted into a red flag for radicalisation. When you consider the ways in which Prevent is, time and time again, disproportionately aimed at Muslims, it becomes clear that not only does society and government manufacture the conditions of our poverty but they also then criminalise us once we get there, creating a double bind which pushes Muslims further into disenfranchisement and alienation and further away from accessing any real, meaningful support when we need it most.

On a community level, too, Muslims are often accused of being insular, not participating in society and not assimilating like other communities. Sections of the right-wing media hyperfixate on Muslims living in ghettos and segregated areas away from the rest of society without any critical analysis on the economic conditions that create a reliance upon social housing amongst parts of the Muslim community or why we are often grouped together in the first place. Hysteria-fuelled disinformation about 'no-go areas' where Muslims rule by Shariah law and attack any dawdling white person finds itself plastered on newspapers and spread through whispers in pubs. We are blamed, further ostracised and looked upon with suspicion and derision for the conditions of our own economic subjugation.

Those in charge are not above using our disproportionate poverty as a way to further demonise us either. In 2016, former chair of the Equality and Human Rights Commission Trevor Phillips claimed that British Muslims were becoming 'a nation within a nation', evoking the long-held far-right fixation on Muslim communities as secret societies leading illicit double lives right under the noses of everyday Britons. As part of this Islamophobic tirade (from a man once tasked with heading the UK's equalities watchdog, no less), he offered the suggestion that schools should have a 50 per cent limit on the number of ethnic minority pupils and that the ethnic composition of council housing should be monitored by the state to stop them becoming 'ghetto villages'. Given that the entire speech was about how Muslims held entirely different views to the rest of society and were fast becoming a separate nation altogether, it barely requires a stretch of the imagination to identify exactly *which* ethnic minorities he is endorsing the capping of in schools and social housing.

Think about this phrase: 'a nation within a nation'. What does it mean? It contains within it the inaccurate assumption that certain communities, like Muslims, themselves have the power to simply *go* independent. It presumes that they are not ostracised from the dominant society: a society that is fundamentally uncomfortable with anyone who doesn't follow its codes and norms.

I've been thinking a lot about what class means for our Muslimness lately as Israel's brutal attack on Gaza continues under the supervision and assent of our western leaders. My first reaction has been to be unapologetic about my support for the Palestinian cause – to post freely on social media, to wear a Palestinian badge on my coat and a 'free Palestine' jumper whilst walking with my toddler in the park. But the reaction of my parents has been one of fear. They might feel the same anger, outrage and heartbreak as me, but their trigger response has been not to rock the boat. Don't put yourself in danger by discussing Palestine in public or wearing your support on your sleeve. Don't make yourself the victim of an attack as Islamophobia continues to soar. I've even heard of Muslim women removing their hijabs in response to the threat of increasing Islamophobia and there are certainly a number of high-profile Muslims who used their public platforms to advocate for Ukraine but have grown deafeningly silent during this latest escalation of the ongoing genocide of the population of Palestine.

There's been a lot written about what it means to be a different class to your roots, to your parents, to where you grew up. Don't get me wrong, as a schoolteacher, it's not as though I've risen to the lofty ranks of wealth and status, but my university education and my designated 'professional' occupation affords me a level of privilege that I know my parents still do not have. It's a strange thing, but only now can I see what it has done to me politically and how it has validated me personally. Throughout my teenage and adult life, I was almost always on the search for a way to be unapologetic. I battled between being palatable, belonging and sticking out for the sake of it. I knew that the hijab was a way to assert my identity, to forge a version of myself that I could feel secure in for once and to find belonging with God where humans had failed me. But what I neglected to realise was the way in which my class identity had the potential to radically change my politics – because your social class is a cushion that allows you to access that unapologeticness and have the privilege to not fear the consequences. This is not because I can afford to lose my job, but rather because my mindset is, mercifully, not one of day-by-day survival. My status (albeit as a cog in the capitalist wheel) affords me at least the luxury of imagining that I am not quite *fully* disposable in this predatory nation that tyrannises dissent.

My parents' fear for me is of course the normal fear of any parent for their child. No matter your politics, parenthood makes you selfish – no one wants *their* own child to become a martyr at the hands of someone with an agenda. But there's something else, too. There's also an element of still existing in that precarity, still feeling that instability that is rooted in the struggle of the working class. For Muslims, this fear becomes one of getting in trouble with the police, losing your job or even getting kicked out of the country altogether if you so much as wear red, green and black to work, share a social media post about genocide or hold political views that don't echo the Prime Minister's, pushing us into silence and disillusionment and ostracising us from civic life altogether.

CHAPTER 9

BOTTOM OF THE CLASS

BEING MUSLIM IN AN EDUCATION SYSTEM THAT EXCLUDES US

The first time I was ever aware of being non-white was in the playground of my primary school. It was lunchtime in early summer and we spent it spinning our gangling bodies around peeling metal infrastructure, drinking in the heady scent of freshly cut grass from the school field and making daisy chains that we'd wear until they wilted away. It was amidst all this that one of my best friends turned to me, nonchalant, and said, 'You have rabies because your dad is from Africa.' Casual. Breezy. Matter-of-fact. As if she'd said, 'You've got some jam on your top, by the way.'

Of course, everyone laughed, because something about the word 'rabies' sounds funny to kids who don't know what it means. Internally, I started a thought process that it had never occurred to me to attempt before. Whatever, whoever, my dad was had some bearing on who I was, too. When, at sports day, classmates asked my brother if our dad was the black footballer Sol Campbell, we thought it was cool. When teachers asked us where our surname came from, we relished in the limelight of being just slightly, still comfortably, different – like that kid who randomly has fifteen pets or claims some distant blood tie to a minor celebrity. The shadows were shifting and suddenly I was seeing things that I'd always thought of as quirks in a different light. It didn't matter that I didn't know what rabies was, or the fact I was sure neither my dad nor I had it. It sounded wrong and dirty. Foreign. Strange enough to send the message that already I didn't belong, already I was different to my friends and the people around me. Already, I was something diseased and sinister.

It was at school, too, where we lay in the sun, the flounces of our red and white checked summer dresses sprawled around us, where a girl in my class asked why the hairs on my legs were black instead of golden like hers. That night, I went home and found an old, rusted razor at the bottom of the bathroom drawer and used it to hack, cut and scour my legs clean of their foreignness. The next day, I went into school excited to suddenly belong, but my legs were now covered in scabs and by the time they healed, I was back to square one.

Years later, it was school, again, where I turned up in a hijab only for a girl I barely knew to tell me she couldn't look at me any more with my head covered like that, for a Muslim girl to ask if I was playing a practical joke and for my favourite teacher to call me Rukshana because she didn't bother to look at my face, just the cloth around it. It was school where a teacher raised an eyebrow and made a joke about my dad forcing me into wearing it. It was a school where a boy asked me if 'we are the ones who shoot everyone', except this time I was at the front of the classroom instead of behind a desk. It was a school where an expert in safeguarding told a hall in which I was the only visibly Muslim teacher that Muslim girls going on holiday to their 'motherlands' needed to be automatically reported to her because they might be on the receiving end of a forced marriage or become a victim of female genital mutilation. It was a school where a picture of Shamima Begum was projected as a reminder that when it comes to Muslim children, we should always start from a place of suspicion or, as the safeguarding expert put it, 'caution'. It was a school where two girls I'd given detention to the day before barged into my classroom whilst I was praying and mocked me whilst I could do nothing but carry on praying. And, you guessed it, it was a packed school hall one evening where a parent quizzed me on whether I even had a degree to teach their child in the first place and *shouldn't English be taught by people who are English?*

School was the place where I learned how to count in French, balance an equation and bake scones. How to make friends, manage my time and read a book. It was also the place where I learned to fold myself up into something palatable, to slot myself into the narrow confines of what is acceptable, what is cool, what belongs.

It's no coincidence that all of these life-defining events occurred in school. By the time a British child is eighteen, they will have spent thousands of hours in school. But it's about more than the sheer amount of time we spend in a classroom. A school is a magnifying glass held up to the world just outside of its gates. We like to think of children as enlightened: bright lanterns guiding our way to a better, more progressive future. But, by and large, children just replicate whatever they see at home. Take whichever stereotypes and barriers that divide our adult lives and you'll see children barely old enough to tie their laces already recreating them, adept at absorbing and perpetuating the prejudices that rule our world before they even know what they mean.

Patriarchy is reenacted on the playground by pressed six-year-old mothers staying home with the imaginary baby all day whilst the infant father goes out and does whatever limitless career they never even fathom fatherhood will stop them fulfilling. Classism seeps into the pores of children too young to name it but old enough to know that the kid with the holes in her shoes and perpetually greasy hair is not the kind of person they want to hang around with. And there's scarcely anything more sobering than hearing a word like 'Paki' encrusted in the lexicon of a child who knows nothing of its weight but, somehow, implicitly understands it as a label that can be applied to little Maryam in their class who took their favourite toy.

But schools also serve a more politicised and pernicious purpose, forming a vital part of the wider liberal infrastructure that dictates what is acceptable and normative in society and what must be educated or policed away.

For this reason, almost every minority finds itself persecuted somewhat within the environment of a school – regardless of how safe, supportive or apolitical schools purport to be. The government is forever using the classroom, curriculum or teachers themselves as an ever-shifting front line for the defining culture wars of our time, from gender ideology to race, nationalism to British values. But for Muslim children, the threat is particularly acute because, at its heart, British education remains not just an endeavour of liberalism but one of liberalis*ing*, and Muslim communities perpetually find themselves on the receiving end of this pursuit. For liberalism to function, it requires there to be liberal values in the first place and then for there to be people who need those values in order to be emancipated – and this is where education falls into the wider political agenda. If bombing liberal values into backward Arabs halfway across the world is on the extreme end of the spectrum, the milder end is what occurs in the classroom.

Since the Education Act of 2002, all maintained schools

have had the duty to promote the spiritual, moral, cultural, mental and physical development of a child. In other words, rather than schools taking a young person for who they are and what they believe in and educating them regardless, schools must instead be proactive in shaping the kind of spirituality and morality, culture and development that they want to see in a child. The government doesn't allow schools to take Britishness as a category of identity in constant flux, to mould to their own student bodies. No, schools are required to teach you what it means to be British and how to be British and to impart knowledge on what sins are unforgivable against the all-powerful deity otherwise known as British values.

In this context, PSHE essentially takes liberal views on sex, relationships and gender and establishes them as the only acceptable norms – the most enlightened and progressive way of living. Science paves the way for dismantling religious gods in favour of secular ones. Citizenship teaches children that ultimate sovereignty lies with the nation state and that the only morals worthy of adherence are British values. The humanities peddle a liberal view of the world in which the only voices worthy of our attention, the only facts that are truly right and the only sources of actual meaningful art are western. Maths, science and business teach us that our manifest purpose is not divine but rather to take up our post at the capitalist wheel.

This is how liberalism is built into the curriculum, but

on an individual level there are many teachers who view it as their own personal teaching philosophy to liberalise the students they teach – whether they are conscious of this intention or not. It is not a design flaw that so many teachers are white – it is built into the very premise of the education system. Such a dynamic is necessary to fuel the ongoing colonial programme: one which schools play a fundamental part in fulfilling. In 2020, just under half of all British schools had no ethnic minority teachers. In fact, whilst white people constitute 80 per cent of the working-age population, 90 per cent of teaching staff are white. For headteachers, the figure sits at 96 per cent. Compare this against the increasingly diverse British population and it exposes how teachers steeped in the power and privilege of whiteness might end up viewing their role of educating black and brown kids as being about far more than just phonics or PE lessons.

I can think of multiple schools with an almost exclusively Muslim student body and overwhelmingly white teaching staff in which teachers barely bother to disguise their agenda to proselytise liberal values onto the inherently archaic Muslim students they teach. Stereotypes which paint Muslim youth as the antithesis to liberal, progressive (read: British) values are prevalent in schools. From assumptions that all Muslim students are homophobic (or homophobic *because* of their religion in a way that other students are not) to the Islamophobic notion that Muslim boys have a problem with female authority not because of twisted ideas about masculinity pervading on social media but because their culture, their religion, their families haven't taught them to respect women. It is commonplace for white teachers in settings like these to deliberately liberalise their teaching, not because their students have displayed any discriminatory views but because their entire method of educating is built upon the presumption that Muslim children *will* hold certain values and that it is their duty to disrupt and aggravate these. I'm all for elevating minority perspectives in the classroom – especially in subjects like English, my own. But I have known teachers to deliberately choose books that cover issues such as LGBT relationships, Jewish characters or women's rights precisely because they think they will be controversial and because they assume that their Muslim students will then share prejudicial ideas that they can pounce on and dismantle in the classroom. At the same time, I have seen instances of the opposite, where classic texts that cover issues such as the Holocaust are avoided in majority Muslim settings because white teachers expect either that Muslims won't relate to Jewish characters or that it will provoke racism from a student body that has been written off as antisemitic simply because of their faith – without any evidence to support that notion.

This matters because it allows ideas about Muslims being backwards and primitive to be enshrined into what and how we teach the next generation. It also means that for

Muslim students, school is not a safe place where they can feel comfortable in their own identities but a place where another, inherently 'better' identity is forcibly transplanted. It matters, too, because what happens at school forms a trajectory for the rest of a person's life. If they are disproportionately punished for behaviour violations because their average teenage defiance is racialised as intimidation, if their professions of faith are treated as evidence of extremism, if their political views are criminalised as radicalisation, if they are penalised for holding values that aren't in sync with the liberal agenda, this warps their future prospects, affects their mental health and disenfranchises them from Britishness altogether. It makes Muslim children unsafe in British classrooms.

Fundamental to the liberal agenda inherent in teaching is the securitisation of Muslims that occurs on school grounds. After 9/11, counter-terrorism came to the forefront of every western nation's mind. Strategies were implemented to infiltrate Muslim communities: FBI agents masquerading as converts, MI5 paying British Muslims to spy on their fellow counterparts, cracking down on so-called hate preachers thought to be spreading conservative or extremist ideologies to mosque congregations. Preventing terror suddenly became a smokescreen to allow every iteration of Islamophobia to pass the dinner-table test. It didn't matter what you did to Muslims as long as you saved one white life on the way.

The UK's response was to develop its CONTEST counter-terrorism strategy, consisting of the 'four Ps': Prevent, Pursue, Protect and Prepare – as though we wouldn't notice that it was a system of demonisation and racism under all that alliteration. It is the most controversial of all the strands, Prevent, that has become a means for policing Muslimness in and of itself in schools, hospitals and public institutions. It is Prevent that makes Muslim students and Muslim teachers subjects of criminalisation in the institutions where they should be safe. It is Prevent that misconstrues mood swings in teenagers for symptoms of radicalisation, that doesn't even allow Muslim toddlers the luxury of mispronouncing words without being referred to counter-terror police, like the four-year-old whose nursery reported him for saying 'cooker bomb' instead of 'cucumber' or another four-year-old who spoke about playing *Fortnite* and his teachers thought he was talking about seeing real weapons.

Since 2015, Prevent has been a statutory duty incumbent upon everyone in the public sector – like teachers, nurses, doctors and social workers. We become the first line of defence against those in our care becoming terrorists or sympathising with extremist ideology. Just like we are vigilant for signs of child abuse or bullying, we are mandated to find ways to support those vulnerable to radicalisation and guide them towards more liberal mindsets – by referring them to Prevent. Despite the fact that today, more referrals concern far-right extremism, from the outset, Prevent has always been designed to tackle the problem of so-called Islamist extremism. At its inception, Prevent was rolled out to the local authorities with the most diverse populations, with more funding going to councils that had more Muslims residents. Now it exists as a crucial and inextricable part of the wider Islamophobia infrastructure that purports to stop terrorism whilst ultimately doing nothing but outlawing Muslimness itself.

The trouble is, Prevent masquerades under the reassuring veneer of safeguarding whilst really being nothing but a vehicle to further monitor and control Muslim communities by criminalising our children. If a teacher is concerned that a student's decision to suddenly wear the hijab, discuss Palestine or ask for a space to pray is indicative of them being radicalised and even on the pathway to terrorism, they are legally obliged (or sometimes moved to by their own misconceptions and prejudices) to make a referral to Prevent. What happens next is that counter-terror officers – often masquerading as something less threatening – will visit the home or school and question the child and sometimes their families. NGOs which monitor Prevent such as Prevent Watch and CAGE repeatedly report that the many cases they see involve children being questioned by counter-terror officers without their parents' consent. Paradoxically, because a person questioned under Prevent legislation is not accused of a crime (this is a pre-crime phase of the counter-terror strategy), they are often stripped of some of the rights a formal arrest may provide them with, such as the right to legal representation or an adult present in the case of children.

The entire premise of Prevent is that it's better to be suspicious than complacent. It's safer to report something and for it to be unfounded than to ignore something that would have actually been significant. On the government's own 'Educate Against Hate' site for schools, it claims that 'you won't ruin lives by making a referral but you might save them', providing teachers with a greater incentive to report any behaviour that could even vaguely be construed as fundamentalism, even if it's something harmless. But this is a fallacy designed to fuel the criminalisation of Muslims and to ultimately serve the policy's surveillance aims. Even children whose referrals dwindle to nothing are left with the evidence on their academic record and on police databases alongside genuine criminals. Prevent Watch outlines how in some cases, past Prevent referrals that came to nothing have cost young people college and university places and have even been shared between police forces in the UK, their data enshrined alongside murderers and rapists simply for the crime of expressing Muslimness in the classroom. What's more, the sheer ordeal of counter-terror officers coming to your door, perhaps in full view of your neighbours, and questioning you about a passing comment made by your young child is itself an incredibly traumatic experience that is likely to have wider consequences on a person's mental health, community and future relationship with authority. To say a referral cannot ruin a life is to pit Muslim lives as meaningless.

Prevent is precisely so dangerous because its vague, paradoxical advice about what to report leaves a void for the prejudices of individual teachers to fill. And in a teaching workforce that is 90 per cent white, those stereotypes are likely manifold.

The fact that most Prevent referrals come through educational institutions exposes the policy as being at its most dangerous and problematic when operating in schools. And, in turn, this gets to the very heart of the question: what functions do we expect our schools to play in our society? To educate, to enlighten, to guide? To be a safe space for students to discover their own identities and make sense of the world around them under the supervision of teachers who are as invested in their pastoral and personal development as they are in their academic achievements? To absorb and deflect the tumults of adolescence and churn out an adult at the end who is ready to function in the real world?

But how can this be guaranteed for Muslim children when teachers are simultaneously primed to read radicalism into harmless teenage angst and extremism into a throwaway comment by a young person who barely understands it? It is one thing to spot extremist tendencies in an adult, but it is another matter entirely to second-guess the behaviour of children in the same way. Sit through any Prevent training (which are regular and mandatory in schools) and you'll see that the so-called risk indicators for radicalisation sound alarmingly like being a moody teenager who spends too much time online. Becoming more isolated socially, having staunch or controversial opinions, experimenting with religious or cultural identities and discussing global politics in class are symptoms of learning how to become an adult. What teenager do you know that isn't reclusive half of the time? What adolescent isn't experimenting with what they wear, how they look and who they are? Kids regularly bring to the classroom the things that they've heard discussed on the news and at home – not because they've been radicalised by a faraway conflict but because they are curious. Policing that curiosity and warping it into a sign of extremism means the erasure of childhood, of innocence, of safety and of security for Muslim students in British schools.

The alarming reality is that things are only getting worse. The year of 2023 saw the long-anticipated independent review of Prevent – whose independence was immediately cast into doubt by the reputation of its author, William Shawcross, who has links to Islamophobic think tanks such as the Henry Jackson Foundation and Policy Exchange and once called Islam 'one of the greatest, most terrifying problems' facing the west. Despite being boycotted by a number of high-profile critics of Prevent, the review nevertheless was published in 2023 and concluded in no uncertain terms that the strategy should stop focusing so much on far-right extremism and redirect its attention on what it terms 'Islamist extremism'. We have been distracted by the far right, apparently. Muslims are and always have been the real problem. The report features a number of problematic claims bandied about by the author with little in the way of evidence. According to Shawcross, Islamism is the idea that Islam forms the centre of your entire identity – a label that applies to most Muslims I can think of. He also lists a number of terrorist attacks that have occurred during his time working on the report, stating that they all 'were Islamist in nature' whilst conveniently missing out instances of far-right terrorism, like the Dover migrant centre bombing in 2022.

A version of Prevent that focuses even more on Muslimness (or so-called Islamism) than it already does signifies nothing but an alarming future awaiting British Muslims. As I finish writing this book, we're seeing this play out in real time in the way that support for Palestine is being policed in schools. As I write, Israel has been waging a two-week-long attack on Gaza's civilians and infrastructure. Israel has cut off Gaza's water and fuel. Millions are homeless. Thousands are dead. Bodies are piling up in the streets and filling ice cream trucks because there is nowhere to put them. Parents are collecting their children's body parts in carrier bags. Babies are witnessing their entire bloodline decimated in a second. I have seen so many images of dead, dismembered and mutilated children that I cannot close my eyes at night without seeing them burned into my vision. Muslim children are seeing this too; every second they're on social media is spent absorbing horrific, graphic and harrowing footage that would be enough to traumatise an adult let alone a child.

The UK government, whilst working hard to sanction the genocide being committed by Israel and stress its unwavering support for Israel's right to defend itself by ethnically cleansing Palestinians, has focused its attention on broadening its criminalisation of Muslims domestically. Newspaper headlines are conflating British protesters with jihadis. The Home Secretary has flirted on a public stage with the idea of outlawing the Palestinian flag. Police officers are turning up at people's doors to question them about pro-Palestine posters in their windows. People are losing their jobs for calling for an end to genocide. And yet, even in all this, one of the government's most vital and indiscriminate frontiers to defend its liberal support for terrorism, as long as it's a western ally doing it, is the classroom.

We are seeing referrals to Prevent for drawing a Palestinian flag on an exercise book, for expressing the idea that the west is complicit in the ethnic cleansing of the entire Gazan populace. We are witnessing children being isolated, excluded or put into detention for standing with Palestine. A letter was recently sent to the headteachers of a number of London boroughs outlining the Met's intention to 'increase intelligence gathering in London schools'. Schools are silencing pupils' voices on the issue and neglecting their duties to safeguard, support and hear the questions, anger and concern of their Muslim pupils who have been exposed to the most unthinkable atrocities towards their siblings in faith. Prevent doesn't just criminalise Muslims – it dehumanises us to the extent that our children are no longer deserving of the same care in schools as other children.

This criminalisation of Muslims cannot be separated from British schooling's wider liberal aims. It's no coincidence that expressing political opinions on Middle Eastern conflicts, showing a 'desire to visit a war zone' (which could form the definition of most Muslim-majority countries) or revealing criticism for western foreign policy are all triggers for Prevent. Liberalism establishes the hypocritical imperatives that some soldiers are heroes, others are terrorists; some wars are noble, others are savage; some violence is justified, whereas some is uncivilised. School is the place where we Muslims must be educated out of our convictions because otherwise we threaten to disrupt the status quo as adults. And that's something Britain never abides.

When I was coming to the end of my degree and

wondering what on earth to do with this not-yet-completed BA in philosophy and literature, I kept putting off what felt like the only viable career option because I wanted to do something *political*. To my mind, this would be something like working in politics, in a think tank or as a journalist. I felt like I had too much anti-establishment anger bubbling up inside of me, too much resistance to do something as *pedestrian* as working with kids. Besides, I had presumed teaching to be the somewhat dowdy career that people do because they want the holidays off with their own children – and it didn't help that well-intentioned relatives kept telling me to go into teaching for that very reason. But all I could picture was primordial history teachers whittling on about the First World War whilst nodding off or spending my life arguing with teenagers about irrelevant uniform violations. I wanted to channel my rage into something bigger.

Ultimately, though, I couldn't escape the fate of most English graduates. I got a place on a teacher training course. And it took me barely one day in the classroom to realise that I was wrong. There's scarcely a more radical, more political act than being a teacher in a classroom. Especially a teacher who, just by being there, disrupts the endless barrage of securitisation and policing aimed at Muslim students.

In many ways, children at the developmental crossroads of their lives, with minds at their most impressionable and feelings at their most volatile, learn how to be adults from the teachers they are exposed to every day. Teachers are held to scrupulous professional standards on how we behave and interact with our students, but it also matters who we *are*. In my seven years of teaching, if I've learned one thing, it's that kids pay attention. Granted, not to the stuff that matters like the task you've just explained for the fourth time. But they remember if you once mentioned when your birthday was. They notice that you usually wear a certain necklace and they'll ask why you're not wearing it that day. They clock that you must be a coffee addict because you drink one during every lesson.

If they take notice of those things, the big things must matter more. They realise that you, the person standing at the front of the classroom, share the same background as them. They notice hints of the same accent, references to a similar upbringing. It makes a difference that you understand that they might be tired because it's Ramadan or that certain global events might ignite personal trauma. It matters that they can see you praying in your classroom at lunchtime because it tells them that Britishness is not monolithic. That religious expression is not shameful or weird. In you, they might see a future version of themselves. That if you can get an education and have a career, they can, too – no matter what societal barriers we have to traverse.

Ethnic minority teachers become a safe space for students to share things that they might struggle to articulate to a teacher who has never experienced racism first-hand. To ask questions that they're too embarrassed to ask a teacher who simply wouldn't get it. Like if they can use your classroom to pray in or whether the meat in the canteen is halal because when they asked the dinner ladies they said, 'No, love, it's not lamb, it's beef' (true story). At the same time, non-white teachers can better advocate for non-white pupils because they know how it feels to be otherised at school. We can push for more inclusive texts, for world history lessons that explore students' own heritage. We can identify where rigid structures need to be more flexible in order to accommodate the diverse needs and experiences of our students because we *were* them, once upon a time.

As a visibly Muslim woman at the front of the classroom, I recognise that flash of recognition in the eyes of my Muslim students when we first meet. When we are so used to seeing Muslim women in the public arena as either victims, perpetrators of terror or domestic-servants-slash-baby-machines, it is revolutionary to identify someone like you in the place you spend your formative years. I still remember the feeling of being taught by a student teacher called Miss Hussain for a term when I was in secondary school. I was so excited to finally have a Muslim teacher that I remember inventing ridiculous ways to weave into conversation that I was Muslim, too. To get to replicate that every day for my students is not just fulfilling; it is political.

It is important. It disrupts the dominant narratives of what society tells us Muslim womanhood should be – meek, mute and separate from the rest of society.

But being a visibly Muslim teacher is not just transformational for my Muslim students. It matters to expose white children as well to the notion that Muslim women are more than just the background noise to everyone else's lives. The school I trained at served what was once Europe's largest council estate. Despite it being merely five minutes from where I grew up, I felt foreign from the start. Because I was. The majority of the students were white and had never spoken to a Muslim adult before apart from the owner of the local corner shop, who was probably a Sikh. Their parents read the *Daily Mail*. I think some of them didn't realise that Muslim women could actually speak – certainly not English anyway. After I had established that I was in fact their teacher and not the cleaner, my first lessons were taken up with ad hoc Q&A sessions made up of entirely innocent, albeit incredibly bizarre, questions – some of my favourite being: am I bald under there, is my hijab pinned straight into my scalp like a pin cushion and doesn't it mean I can't hear anything because my ears are covered?

As it happens, I'm sure many of the other teachers were baffled by the sight of me, too. On my induction day, the outgoing head of English rather awkwardly quizzed me on my ethnic origins and then, oddly, proceeded to ask me what foods I ate as a child with a look of such discomfort on his face that I ended up making something up just to put him out of his misery. My mentor asked me if my plan was to stay in the school long term or get my qualification and then 'f*ck off to Saudi Arabia or wherever'. I was profusely reassured that he wasn't racist, he was just very Scottish.

What message does it send to white children if they are only ever taught by white adults? That only white people have the expertise to educate the next generation? That it is only the authority of white people that they need to adhere to? That only white people contribute to society? It certainly might not feel like it when reprimanding a student for the umpteenth time about not completing their homework, but hidden in that small act is a radical life lesson. It is teaching them that people who look, sound and believe differently to them don't just matter but can be authority figures, too. That, no matter how racism still pervades in the world today, our voices must and will be heard and that power should be earned, not sewn into one's skin.

But if teaching as a visibly Muslim woman is important, teaching English as a Muslim woman is a whole other level of responsibility. And even more of a political act. Literature, publishing, media and the arts remain overwhelmingly dominated by the white and the privately educated. Studies have found that over half of UK journalists attended fee-paying schools compared to around 7 per cent of the general population and that just under 90 per cent are white. The arts are made up of those rich enough to embark on creative pursuits whilst having a handy little trust fund to keep them more than afloat. Lots of children think these disciplines simply aren't for them. In this context, it's tough to get kids to see English as a valuable life skill or a door to a career that could ever be within their reach. It's little surprise that A-level English take-up is plummeting nationally year on year when English is viewed as a folly rather than a route to anywhere meaningful.

Take a look at the staff breakdown of any British secondary school and you'll almost always find that the few ethnic minority teachers (if there are any) are the preserve of the science and maths departments – especially outside of London. English departments, by and large, still resemble the lightest end of the Dulux colour chart, ranging from about snow to off-white. The extent of diversity might be some dyed pink hair, and you'd be forgiven for thinking owning brogues, a tote bag and a National Trust membership were prerequisites of a PGCE in English.

When English teachers don't look like the kids they teach, don't come from their backgrounds or empathise with their worldview, students miss out on what the subject can offer. And in our modern day, young people need more than ever a safe space to make sense of the defining issues of our time, through literature and debate. The curriculum may already be dominated by stale, pale men, but if your entire English department has no personal experience with otherisation, it robs students of that rare, heady joy of recognising yourself in a book or a poem.

The few moments I saw myself reflected on the page in my English lessons are still etched in my mind because they left such an indelible mark on my sense of self. I painstakingly extrapolated the poem 'Presents from My Aunts in Pakistan' to apply to me because I had never before seen myself on the page. In my mind, it became 'Presents from My Aunts in Libya', swapping references to salwar kameez to jalabiyas, Lahore for Benghazi. I had never before witnessed the unpacking of everything I felt, of being torn between two versions of myself, neither one nor the other, in something we studied at school. It was my first real realisation that I wasn't alone. When I studied *Othello* in Year 12, I became fixated on the eponymous character's ambiguous North African origins. Our teacher explained that the label 'moor' referred to the region I spent all of my summers, and so starved was I of representation that I felt exhilarated that Shakespeare had written about someone like me. Even if he wasn't like me at all, but a man racialised as violent, primitive and animalistic. Even if the play is dripping in racist tropes. I was so enrapt at our imagined cultural connection that it eclipsed everything else.

When calls are made to decolonise the curriculum, critics often ask what we would do with the classics written by those very pale, stale men that have fallen out of favour now. But diversifying our schools isn't about burning the texts written by white men and replacing them with diaspora poets. Not all of them anyway. If we want the education system to reflect our changing world, for it to acknowledge the Britain of today and not a century ago, that means diversifying teaching itself. Particularly subjects like English. If our educators come from a range of backgrounds, if they understand what it means to be marginalised, we bring that to the texts we teach. We can read between the lines of the status quo, pick up on the unspoken nuances in the same books we've studied for years, critically engage with their message, grapple with their whiteness rather than getting rid of them altogether. When I teach my students literature, I want them to open the book and see themselves right there on the page, humanised and valid enough to be immortalised in literature rather than excluded from it. And doing that, day in, day out, within a nation that tries to fetter me in stereotype, is a quietly radical act.

CHAPTER 10

SALAAMS AND SMILES

WHAT THE HIJAB GAVE ME

When I was seventeen, I got my first pair of Doc Martens. On an icy morning in that lull between Christmas and New Year when there's nothing to do but finish the Quality Street and wonder what day it is, my parents drove me to the factory outlet store on the edge of Northampton; it paid to grow up in the shoe capital of the world. I braced myself to find only luminous green boots and size 12s, but there they were: a pair of classic black 1460s in my size, and thanks to an almost invisible loose thread, they were mine for only £40. I was so excited to wear them that I put them on in the car and then I wore them every day until they wore through.

A few years earlier, I had woken up on a very different kind of morning: a sun-dappled one where the air was thick as treacle and carried the perfume of the jasmines outside. Then, too, I put on a garment and never (in public) removed it again. Except, unlike those Doc Martens which had the luxury of simply remaining shoes, my hijab became a part of me. Yes, it dominated how others saw me and eclipsed all other aspects of my identity, but something else happened, too. Something inside of me. Like an implanted organ, it wove itself into the tissue of my being, beating alongside my heart, and became an immovable part of the person I am.

My relationship with my hijab reminds me in many ways of those Doc Martens because as far as shoes go, they're about as political as you can get. Their history is a tapestry of war and skinheads, punk and socialism. And the hijab, too, is the most controversial garment in the world. Scarcely anyone is entirely impartial about it. And yet, political connotations or not, nobody defines me by the shoes I wear on my feet. Thankfully, I am not presumed to be some sort of modern-day neo-skinhead in a hijab because I reach for a pair of Doc Martens almost every day of my life. Why then, is such weight attached to this other garment – the one on my head? Why is it that entire societies and governments formulate policies and legislation on the assumption that the hijab is a symbol of repression or extremism and not simply a garment like anything else?

The answer lies in humanity. The humanity Muslim women are denied and the humanity everyone else is allowed to have. We presume someone's footwear to be a free choice based on taste, style and comfort rather than some overarching political agenda because we see them as human enough to have whims, likes and pleasure to begin with. Muslim women, on the other hand, are so entrapped in the multiple paradoxical stereotypes that define us that our humanity falls by the wayside altogether. We are always an object – no matter whose victim or whose enemy we are – and that means we can't possibly possess things like joy or fulfilment. And objects can't make choices; certainly not ones that matter.

We don't often hear about the hijab in terms of joy. I'm certainly so used to defending my choice with politicised, unapologetic language that it feels almost indulgent – frivolous and even a little infantilising – to talk about it 'sparking joy', as though the hijab isn't the most contested garment in the world, as though I'm naive to the meaning it holds beyond being just a piece of chiffon or jersey. Besides, it sounds preposterous, and more than a little cliché, to say that a single garment can make up the bulk of the person you are. I am not just a floating head scarf – I'm a mother and a wife, a daughter and a sister, a teacher, a writer, a friend. A coffee addict and embarrassingly addicted to *The Office* (US only). I am a Muslim – even when I take my hijab off at home. The things that I am are neither defined by nor confined to the scarf on my head. And, anyway, hasn't this entire book been about proving that Muslim women are more than pieces of cloth, imploring the public to look beyond their Islamophobic notions to see us as complex and multifaceted human beings?

But articulating our joy is radical when what society says about the hijab is not the same as what we say: we who wear it day in, day out. Part of erasing our humanity is to erase our joy – the meaning we derive from and the delight we find in what everyone else is too busy seeing as our oppression. Perhaps you think us incapable of procuring shards of light in what you see as our prison cell. Maybe you think us so threatening and perverse that you are suspicious of our capacity for joy in the first place – we're too busy plotting the next terror attack or giving birth to more extremist children. But if the din of stereotype ceases just briefly, there's room to see that it's not all objectification and criminalisation, invisibility and paradox. There's community and purpose, jubilance and beauty in this garment that some want to ban and others look to burn.

There is something rare and beautiful in walking down a street and sharing a 'salaam' and a smile with a passer-by because they recognise you as a fellow Muslim. Of walking into a new workplace or classroom and gravitating towards another visible Muslim because your shared identity provides a safe space, a chime of understanding. I can't help but be in awe of girls in Air Force 1s and sweeping abayas sipping iced coffees and discussing their coursework – subconsciously, unknowingly, effortlessly embodying the confidence to be British and to be Muslim in a way that

I'm still not sure I've achieved, even now on the cusp of my thirties.

Wearing the hijab is joyful because it is community. It is memes about that black scarf we wear every day getting side-eyed by the other neglected colours in the wardrobe. It is jokes about grabbing whatever random garment is within reaching distance when the postman comes to the door, like a pair of trousers or a baby's vomit-stained muslin cloth. It is knowing that we have all been asked something ridiculous at some point in our lives about whether we sleep in our hijabs or what will happen if we accidentally show our hair. It is to be plunged into the depths of the valley between misogyny and Islamophobia, between being someone's enemy and someone else's fetish, an object of derision and something to be saved, and amongst it all finding solidarity, finding sisterhood. And of all the things the hijab has given me, sisterhood is pretty high up the list.

The Hijabi's Guide to Making Friends
1. Find yourself in a white-dominated environment. You know the sort: all small talk is about the pub and people ask what school you went to because they regularly forget that not every school is a world-renowned institution haunted by the ghosts of sixty former Prime Ministers. The kind of place where people unnecessarily elongate all the syllables in your name and ask if you went to the temple at the weekend. It's probably run by someone

who calls themselves self-made because they invested Daddy's millions wisely at the age of twenty-one. You get the gist. This sort of place shouldn't be difficult to find – it will probably be every job you ever have in your whole adult life.
2. If you're lucky, there will be one other hijabi there – possibly in a different department, maybe on a different floor. She might have worked there for years and grown jaded from all the arranged marriage jokes. Maybe she's succumbed and started calling herself Kate because she got tired of everyone mispronouncing Khadija.
3. Smile at her. She'll smile back, hopefully. And that's it: friends for life. Just be warned – everyone will probably think you're the same person until they see you sitting together at lunch.

There's a reason all of my best friends are hijabis, why my Instagram feed is full of hijabi women sharing modest outfits and hijab styles, Muslim mothers embodying Islamic gentle parenting, Muslim female writers and Muslim female bookstagrammers sharing the words of other… Muslim women. None of this is the work of an algorithm or fate. Whether consciously or not, I have carved a small corner of the world for myself in which, for once, everyone looks like me – and that's because being around other Muslim women feels like therapy in a world that seeks to constantly define, save or control us. It feels both radical and refreshing to be around other women who just *get it*: the juxtaposed dualities of our existence, the restlessness of being hypervisible everywhere we go.

Each of my most cherished friendships is borne of an instantaneous connection, a shared experience of otherness. They are the mementos of a life lived searching for that glitter of familiarity in someone else's eye. A reminder that the whirlwind bonds you forge in isolation are the ones that burrow themselves deepest in your heart. My best friends are not the ones I sat next to for seven years straight at school because our surnames bound us together or who studied the same degree as me. They are the ones who knew what it was like to be the only *other* and waded through it alongside me. They are the ones who came along with me, our palms clammy from nerves, to ask our headteacher for a space to pray; our friendship sealed as we bowed down side by side, hips knocking together in the tight space between the desk and the door and hoping nobody looked through the window to see us doing something as bizarre as praying. They are the ones who, whilst everyone else went clubbing for the fifth night in a row, sat and drank hot chocolate with me and binge-watched our favourite shows. They are the ones who felt the same self-consciousness and imposter syndrome at being surrounded by white skin and posh accents. Who didn't even need to articulate that feeling because we recognised our own fears reflected back at us. It is only by being a hijabi – by wearing my authentic self on my sleeve (or rather, my head) – that these friendships could have blossomed.

Over the last decade and a half, my hijab has meant different things to me at various points. If you'd have asked me at fifteen what the hijab meant to me, I'd have said it was about identity. I had tried being white and it wasn't working out. If there is one thing a girls' school is ruled by, it's cliques, and I had my eyes on the table that the entire school referred to as 'Asia' (yep, overt 2000s racism for you). Being mixed race had taught me that despite what I thought, everything is a dichotomy: you can never really be two things at once. I had never truly been English and Libyan, native and foreign, white and brown at the same time. I had just flitted between the two in different contexts. And when whiteness was done with me, it was time to try out the *other* side. And the only way I could signpost this was proving it through the way I dressed. In the naive, simplified way that only a child can think, I expected it to bring me belonging. It was the ticket to the new me.

Although I was unaware of it at the time, it strikes me as significant that I chose to wear the hijab at precisely the age where womanhood appears over the horizon, where we teeter on the brink of adulthood and ready ourselves to play the role. Being a girl at this age felt like the ground shifting under your feet – your body suddenly blossoming into something with promise, a tool to be cultivated, something to be maintained and nourished rather than just a vessel to get you around. Nobody ever taught me this was the case but all you had to do was open a magazine or a newspaper, watch TV for about thirty seconds or consider what every protagonist in every rom-com looked like and the truth would smack you square in the stomach. The only way to be a woman was to be beautiful. And the only way to do that was to resemble a cross between a Barbie doll and a stick insect. And of course my friends and I inhaled this as gospel, because what are beauty standards if not sheer indoctrination?

The truth was undeniable to me that I wasn't what my friends were, that I wasn't what womanhood was *supposed* to be. I wasn't thin and I didn't have long, flowing blonde hair or glassy, rosy skin or spend my weekends sunbathing in hotpants. I didn't inhabit that spectral, coveted realm of *femininity* like I felt my friends did. I spent my entire evenings plucking my eyebrows to match the litheness of my classmates' and learned the harsh way that no amount of counting calories and skipping meals can condense your bones into something smaller, into something better.

I hadn't simply failed at being white in a political sense – I had failed physically, too. I had failed the test at conception, when I hadn't inherited the right genes. And then I found the hijab. Or it found me. And in it there was not just a portal to a new identity – there was also a way to circumvent the Eurocentric beauty standards that my biology was failing to hold up against.

The first iterations of myself as a hijabi represented an egg. My scarf was wrapped so tight around my head that my face threatened to burst its seams. I didn't have a new wardrobe to match my newly hijabified self, so I was an egg sweating profusely in five different layers. But then I discovered the world of hijabi YouTubers who were coming into their prime just when I needed them most to release me from the chokehold the egg-hijab style had on me. Suddenly, I went from spending my evenings plucking myself into something new to wrapping and rewrapping and re-rewrapping scarves around my head in different styles, creating entirely new looks with a flick of a wrist and a twist of fabric. I pioneered ways to use my old headbands as hijab accessories, clipping bows that once held back a heavy emo fringe onto layers of my intricate cloth origami.

I was never going to match up to Eurocentric ideals that my DNA was rigged against. But by wearing the hijab, it was almost as though I was opting out of that system altogether. Refusing, in my own way, to buy into the male gaze we were already being trained for in our adolescence. It was like, by othering myself, I no longer held myself to the standards that had weighed me down before. To the outside world, this might have looked like I was simply hiding my angst behind my hijab. To me, I thought it was about the politics of identity. But I look back now and realise that what I experienced can only be described as that first taste of the sweetness of true faith – of *imaan*. Of judging myself by the standards of a God who looks in our hearts rather than a society that inspects our bodies.

Perhaps that's why I persevered with the hijab, against all odds, as this not-quite-English, not-quite-Libyan, not-really-Muslim-yet girl. Because for all the darkness, rejection and subjugation that there was during this time, there were fragments of incandescent, illuminating light breaking through, too. I now looked frumpy in comparison to my friends, but I didn't care. For all the teachers who made vaguely hidden racist comments or called me by the wrong name, there were those who complimented my hijab style and asked me about its meaning. Some of my friends wanted nothing to do with me, but others wanted me to wrap hijabs around their heads, too, to test it out – even going home to their likely horrified parents wearing one of my scarves in an opulent turban. I felt empowered and oddly untouchable despite being more hypervisible than I'd ever been in my life, as though my hijab was a forcefield around me. The heady feeling of, finally, being not a failed version of something else but something *new* and exclusively mine had me going to school each day with multiple uniform violations woven into whichever overly ornate hijab style I was donning that day, and no teacher dared question me because it might be construed as racism. I was high from the novelty of it: for the first time, being free from floundering in whiteness and navigating new waters instead. We are so used to articulating the hijab in terms of control and domination, subjugation and invisibility, but this was the first time I ever felt whole – ever felt like someone whole rather than a person in pieces.

In some ways, it worked. I only had to look around the faces of fellow passengers on the bus to see that I had certainly made a success of othering myself. Eventually, though, I realised I was playing at being a hijabi just as much as I had been playing at being white – focused on the outwardly aesthetics of it whilst still not knowing what it really *meant*. I felt subversive, daring, unapologetic, but it was just like cutting a fringe or getting my nose pierced; it made me look different but had done nothing to quieten my internal questions, soothe my inner angst. Yet.

Really, I did things the wrong way round. I wore the hijab before I properly prayed, fasted or read the Qur'an, whereas for most women, the hijab comes as one of the last steps in their spiritual journey: when they feel ready for their exterior to match their personal religious growth. But doing things backwards left me floundering. When people asked me what this scarf meant and why I wore it, I barely knew what to say. When friends' parents asked me over dinner what the difference between Islam and Christianity was, I stuttered and mumbled something incoherent until they moved on. Still, the questions and probing came and the lonely pit inside of me grew. I wasn't enough for this identity either. The two things I was cancelled each other out – being perpetually *both* left me simply being *nothing*.

The hypervisibility of the hijab forced me to rewind and fill in the gaps that I had done a massive leap over. I asked Google all of the questions I had. Yahoo! Answers became my religious guide. From strangers on the internet with usernames like hijabisister786, I learned what others grow up absorbing. I taught myself to read Arabic through YouTube videos intended for converts and listened to Islamic lectures incessantly, pursuing spiritual highs like others seek chemical ones.

The object of my identity shifted from the hijab itself to the God who I now knew, who I now believed ordained it – and to the faith that embedded it as part of its value system. Proving myself as a *real hijabi* turned into something else. Into finding that the gnawing loneliness and ceaseless quest for belonging that had been inside of me since childhood wasn't to be found in socially constructed racial categories or cultures that I would always be a little too *other* for. I realised that what I had been searching for was spiritual belonging. My biology would always stop me from ever being fully white or fully brown, my DNA would never allow me to be solely English or solely Libyan. But there *was* one identity I could solely inhabit. Unadulterated, untainted. And that was being Muslim. The hijab was a vehicle, not the final destination.

But as I waded through to the other side of that

hormone-fuelled malaise called adolescence, my relationship with the hijab took on a political dimension, too. I was no longer seeking permission. No more was I interested in slotting myself into the restrictive preordained slats that society had created for me. My teenage years had been wasted trying to wear whatever my friends were wearing but adding a covered head to the mix. Skater skirts over jeans, T-shirts with long-sleeve tops underneath. Layers and layers and layers to hide who I really was. But once I recognised the politics of being coerced into assimilation, and how it had been working its dark magic on me since birth, it made me unapologetic. And angry. I sought to make myself even more identifiably Muslim. I became brazen in my overt Muslimness in the white spaces I inhabited like my literature and philosophy course at university, where white skin and a private education were practically entry requirements. I ditched jeans and wore abayas, stopped wearing make-up for a time. If someone asked where I was from, I erased the white side altogether. I was Libyan. Muslim. I rejected Britishness entirely because it had first rejected me. I told myself that despite growing up eating Turkey Twizzlers, watching CITV and having all of my cultural references derived from this small island, I was no longer British. My deliberate Muslimness was my way of doubling down on my status as *other*. Reclaiming the stereotypes that fuel our system and saying, *so what?* Declaring my undeniable and immovable existence as in spite of Britain and not part of it. Refusing to cower in the shadows and wait for someone to save me.

With time, I realised that living as a political symbol is, in many ways, as dehumanising as changing yourself to acquiesce. It is exhausting to constantly prove a point. Turning your existence into some big counterpoint to the status quo just cements the same hierarchies that you are trying to protest. Being relentlessly unapologetic might mean refusing to submit, but it means acknowledging that you, in fact, don't belong in the first place. Even if you are refusing to do anything about it. In truth, I was angry with Britain. Like a spurned lover who fuels heartbreak into fury, I wanted to be the one to turn my back on my home. It didn't have the right to do that to me. I hadn't considered that by denying my Britishness, I was feeding into the Islamophobic agenda – that we are perpetually foreign, even if we are born here.

Maybe it's the weight of adulthood, the ceaseless demands of motherhood or the reality of being a cog in an indiscriminate capitalist system, but these days I don't think about my hijab that much at all. OK, I've written a whole book about it. But my intentions for wearing it are no longer rooted in sending a message or inhabiting a particular identity. There's something reassuring, these days, about being content that God has ordained this for my own benefit and leaving it at that. The rejection of the male gaze; the discarding of fast fashion's fickle whims; demanding to be seen as a person and not a body; reasserting my presence in a nation that seeks to reject us: those things are all secondary now. When our modern society worships the ego as God, it can sound almost infantilising to admit to simply following orders. But it really is as simple as that. I feel liberated now knowing I wear this because I believe God told me to – free to live my life unshackled from the pressure of constantly, incessantly proving a point.

The Arabic word 'hijab' translates as 'barrier' or 'covering'. For that reason, it is often seen as antithetical to think of the hijab as a garment of beauty because, by nature, it is intended to conceal beauty – or to reserve it for those with permission to view it, those who already know that your appearance is more than the sum of your parts. Women who wear make-up with the hijab or style it in particularly flamboyant ways are often faced with the accusation that they are going against the meaning of hijab, viewing it as a fashion accessory rather than an object to preserve modesty. But whether or not the hijab is beauti*fying*, it is certainly beauti*ful* in manifold ways. When detached from its narrow political connotations, modesty *is* undeniably and universally beautiful. The beauty icons of the past – from Audrey Hepburn to Sophia Loren, Elizabeth Taylor to Grace Kelly – all dressed in ways that would be considered conservative by today's standards, including longer-length sleeves, midi skirts and even headscarves. Both recently and historically, modesty has always been associated with elegance, luxury and status – consider how, the world over, female monarchs and royals wear clothes that conceal their forms. The most iconic designs from fashion-defining figures like Coco Chanel and Christian Dior wouldn't be amiss on a catwalk dedicated to modest fashion today. Even if feminism has all but cancelled the word for being inherently patriarchal, modesty has always been associated with opulence, affluence and prestige. Today, trends such as 'quiet luxury', which have gained popularity through social media, essentially recreate what religious codes of modesty are so often criticised for – particularly when in a Muslim context. Muted tones, long overcoats over loose trousers, midi dresses and maxi skirts. Even the winter staple of 2023, the balaclava, is frankly nothing but a knitted hijab. Cool on Becky, oppressive on Bushra. When Muslim women dress this way, the default stance of societies and governments is to assume we have been coerced into it. To create policies that limit our access to garments that line the shelves of every high-street store. When everyone else does it, it's chic and fashion conscious. Presumably, because other women are capable of making autonomous bodily decisions whereas Muslim women are not.

It's not just prestige that has long been equated with modesty. More recently, covering one's body has increasingly been considered a marker of aesthetic subversiveness and outlandish unconventionality in the fashion world. Take the now memeified Doja Cat and her all-red jewel-encrusted look that left only her eyeballs uncovered. Or Kim Kardashian's 2021 Met Gala ensemble – an all-black half-unitard, half-niqab that rendered her faceless altogether. A$AP Rocky turning up to practically every red carpet dressed as your average Muslim grandma or Lady Gaga obscuring her entire body with meat or Sia's face hidden with an impossibly long fringe. When the standard position is secular and when the default gaze is white, it's little wonder that the very same garments can hold such divergent political weights, but it does expose how prevalent and hypocritical the double standards around modesty are. Always, always, when it comes to Muslim women covering our bodies, the same restrictive narratives persist. When it's Muslim women who are covered, we are veiled threats roaming the streets of Britain, threatening to blow up whatever stands in our way whilst also, simultaneously, being victims trapped in a cloth prison. But when it's an A-list celebrity or a fashion icon? It's a revolution.

But modesty is not just aesthetic. It has practical implications, too. You only need to rewind a couple of years to the height of the pandemic to see that covered faces and unexposed skin can be more than a religious symbol. The accusation most often put to niqab-wearing Muslim women is that in order to function in a civilised society, we need to see each other's faces. That for security and safety reasons, faces must be identifiable. That nobody can be free, can truly be themselves, if nothing is visible but their eyes. And yet, overnight, what did the world adjust to? We learned to navigate in a world where half of everyone's faces were obscured. Doctors treated patients wearing hazmat suits so extensive that you couldn't make out who was behind them. The situation itself was frightening, but not being able to see the mouth of the person serving you wasn't threatening in the way that niqabi women are accused of being. Yes, it was strange, but we just dealt with it because we afford ourselves enough humanity to accept that the underlying premise for covering our faces is acceptable, that the decision is our own (even if, ironically, this *was* being mandated by a government). And yet, we both infantilise and deride Muslim women to such an extent that we fail to consider that their own reasonings for covering their faces or hair can hold any weight at all. Regardless of how anti-Covid conspiracy theorists are ridiculed, their same narrow and illogical conclusions are perpetuated in society at large when it comes to Islam, and especially in relation to women's rights. If conspiracy theorists believe Covid to be an invention and a means of control, so too does the British public view our agency as a mythical idea that we Muslim women buy into whilst lacking the capacity to realise we are being controlled by some faraway evil force. The pandemic-era symbol of a covered face transcended mere necessity, though. In the first fashion month to take place after consecutive lockdowns brought the industry to a halt, an entire fashion show was built around that iconic image of an obscured face. Paco Rabanne's edit in 2020 featured chainmail covering the whole body (a metal niqab, by any other name). Britain and Europe, it seems, have no trouble adopting a covered face as an archetype when the dictating deities are scientific or stylistic rather than religious.

But in our ever-more surveilled world, obscuring your identity in public is a growing marker of political defiance, too. As long as it's a white person doing it, that is. Britain is widely accused of being the most surveilled country on earth – and whether at protests, when passing CCTV cameras or when asked to be photographed for ID purposes, more and more people are using the obstruction of their identity to send a political message that governments don't have an inherent right to access us, whether it be our bodies, our data or our identities. But whilst politically progressive groups are seen as subversive for covering their faces in this way, Muslim women embodying this same message and applying it to the male gaze are still seen as primitive.

What better summarises that paradox that binds us as Muslim women? That our choices are never good enough, never progressive or sufficiently liberal enough to pass the test of Great Britishness. This once bothered me. I craved the day my decision to cover my hair and body would be accepted, rather than seen as an abrogation of my Britishness entirely. But that day never came, will never come. Being perpetually hypervisible and otherised everywhere you go can provoke you to look for the thin shards of acceptance wherever you find them and mistake them for belonging. I have learned to untangle that feeling of empowerment that I still feel when wearing the hijab from the fascination of white teachers, compliments from my friends or that random white lady who says 'what a gorgeous head scarf!' and instead connect it to something immovable instead: Allah. Wearing the hijab to spite the white gaze is still accepting that whiteness is default, after all. It was never wise or healthy to base my entire existence on the whims of whiteness, because for all the compliments, there are the insults, too. For all the curiosity, there is the derision, too. And if you live in anticipation of one, you open the floodgates to let it all rule your life. Our liberal system which deifies the nation state as god won't tell you this, but Muslim women have the right to derive the meaning of our lives from something other than the society, the state, the system that benefits only from our downfall.

CONCLUSION

I have learned that seeking to slot myself into nationalistic borders is a fruitless pursuit. That trying to belong amidst a system of structural inequality that negates one part of me by virtue of the other existing is a waste of my time. I no longer want to be English or Libyan, white or brown or mixed or any of it. I once bought into the political answers to this question of who I am, who I have permission to be. I believed in anti-racist notions of reclaiming my identity, defining myself by my own standards. In celebrating being othered. But nowadays, I know that no answer, no cure for our eternal quest for belonging can be found in a world so regimented, so dictated by race, class and gender.

Being a Muslim is the only thing I have ever fully, truly been with my entirety. It is the only category I have all the credentials to inhabit, and that is why I am no longer willing to rummage around in the rubbish of what nation states and human movements say I am allowed to be. As colonised people, marginalised people, persecuted people, we have for too long had our personhood dictated by government agendas and social expectation. If a lifetime spent trying to find somewhere to belong has taught me anything, it is that neither whiteness nor otherness is my home. I never belonged in either because I was never meant to be defined by fictional, nationalistic, convenient categories that serve everyone's aims but my own. The only freedom I have found is in rejecting all of that and thinking of myself as not Libyan, not English, not this, not that. Just a Muslim.

That's not to say that we should succumb to the political conditions that subjugate us, nor that we should be apolitical altogether. But why not dream bigger? Why not aim higher? As Audre Lorde put it, the master's tools will never dismantle the master's house. If we define ourselves using only the vocabulary given to us by those who have no interest in our liberation, we get no further than the limits they dictate for us. There is no representation to be found in structures built to exclude us, no liberation in systems designed to divide and rule.

In this book, I've written a lot about yearning for a place I could belong, how that journey shaped and defined my childhood and adolescence, how it led me to the hijab as a way of adopting an identity I could hide behind or discover myself within, or both. But I have come to realise that true resistance is making my existence uncomfortable, is to ruffle feathers and shatter narratives, not to prove a point, not to defy stereotypes but to assert myself. To say, I – we – are here to stay.

I no longer apologise for my presence in this nation whose bloody political past bore my very existence. I no longer view my politics through the lens of proving my humanity. A country like Britain dictates absolute acquiescence to its cues and rules, and if hostile domestic politics and aggressive foreign policy tell us anything, it's that the state fears and despises those who refuse to toe the line. It views those who hold Islam at the centre of their identities as 'Islamists', Muslims whose morals are formed by their faith as extremists, those whose politics are inspired by their Islam as terrorists. Muslim parents who want greater control over what their children learn at school are outcast as bigots. Muslim kids who talk about Palestine in their classrooms are criminalised. The liberal agenda of the state is to eradicate Muslimness entirely, to paint us in the colours of the Union Jack and then applaud itself for how diverse our nation is without ever having to suffer the inconvenience of a true diversity of opinion or belief.

Now I view my existence through the paradigm of resistance. Let our presence in this nation be a reminder that all the colonisation, all the subjugation, all the marginalisation in the world cannot rid Britain of us, cannot wash its hands of the unwanted fruit of its own grimy labours. Let them view me, let them view us, as a veiled threat because, after all, our very presence in this land is a threat to the status quo.

ACKNOWLEDGEMENTS

First and foremost, I thank and praise Allah, the One from whom I came and the One to whom I will return one day. I know that without the blessing and guidance from Him, and without the conviction of my faith, this book would have been nothing but fleeting fragments of ideas immortalised in the notes app on my phone. I pray this book can provide a service for our Muslim community and stir the hearts of those who gain from our further subjugation.

Without my best friend, soulmate and husband, this book would be a half-abandoned project shoved in a drawer somewhere. To my Umar, I am more grateful than I can ever say for the way in which you have always believed in my writing and my story with more conviction than me. For the late nights spent agonising over specific phrasing, the hours of proofreading and brainstorming and the trips to book shops to remind me that one day my book too will be on those shelves. For being my biggest support, my kindest critic and as invested in this as if it was your own: thank you.

To my baby, my A. The one who made me a mother. My heart in human form. I hope you're proud of your mama.

To my beautiful and selfless parents who gave us everything they had even when it meant going without themselves, working longer hours or sacrificing something else. Thank you for every sleepless night, every twinge of pain and every pang of worry. You are the best parents I could have been blessed with and I am who I am because of everything you have always done: all you invested, toiled and surrendered. There is a reason they say you can never fully appreciate your parents until you become one yourself. I hope I can be even half the parent you have both been to me.

Lastly, to my wonderful agent Amberley Lowis who contacted me out of the blue when I was in the middle of a tumult of dirty nappies and cluster feeding (otherwise known as maternity leave) and asked me whether I'd ever considered writing a book – to which I replied that I had rarely thought of anything else but had no idea how to make it actually happen. That serendipitous moment is what brought us here today and without your belief in me, and your unwavering conviction in amplifying marginalised

ACKNOWLEDGEMENTS

voices, I'd still be whiling away my time dreaming of someday becoming a published author. Thank you for taking a chance on me and for being the agent that I always needed but hadn't a clue how to look for.